ALL ABOUT
WINES & SPIRITS
plus
HOW TO MIX
1000 COCKTAILS

Contents

Contents (Continued)

Wines

Champagne

True champagne is made only from grapes grown in the old Province of Champagne in the northeast corner of France, just north of Burgundy and west of Alsace. It is today known as the Department of the Marne. This department is broken up into four distinct divisions, namely: the district around the city of Reims, that of the town of Ay and adjacent localities north of the Marne, that of Epernay south of the river, and that of the Côte d'Avize stretching towards the southeast.

In these areas mentioned there are over 30,000 acres under cultivation. Of the 30,000 acres of vineland in the sparkling wine district divided among 17,000 proprietors, over 2,500 acres belong to the Moet & Chandon firm. The champagne vineyards in total are valued at over $30,000,000 and are attended by more than 35,000 vine dressers.

Wines produced in other wine-producing districts of the world and even in the United States have been labeled champagne, but in the true sense of the word, only wine made in the French Department of the Marne is champagne and should be called champagne. If the wine is produced in France and is labeled champagne, the cork itself will have the name "Champagne" imprinted upon it. This is an additional protection to the practical impossibility of imitating the fine quality and flavor along with the other incomparable characteristics.

Champagne is not a cheap wine because of the high taxes and duties, and because it takes so long to prepare it for market. It is and always has been the wine of luxury. A person drinking champagne should be willing to pay a good price for this wine since the cheaper champagnes will probably be inferior final pressings after the first good wines have been pressed out, or else the raw, crude produce of unfavorably situated vineyards of the lowest category.

Grape vines have been cultivated in Champagne since time immemorial, but up to the close of the seventeenth century only red and white still wines had been produced. Although the discovery of sparkling wines has been credited to Dom Perignon, head cellarer of the Abbey of Hautvillers, sparkling wines had been made before he was born. Champagne of the modern fashion, however, was originated by Dom Perignon about the year 1670. He supervised the care of the vines and the making of the wine. Some time later, it occurred to him to "marry" wines of various qualities, the produce of the different

7

vineyards together, in order to secure a sound standard of excellence. He also succeeded in making white wine from black grapes and by some means found a method of regulating the tendency of champagne to effervesce.

By paying particular attention to the period best suited for bottling, he succeeded in producing a perfectly sparkling wine which leapt forth from the bottle and overflowed the glass. Further, Perignon contrived to clear or fine the wine without decanting it from one bottle into another. He also received credit for being the first to use the bark of the cork tree as a stopper for the bottle instead of the bits of tow dipped in oil or tallow.

There are four principle champagne vines, three of the Pineau variety, so called because the grapes, black in color, cluster in the conical form of the pine. They include the "Franc Pineau," whose fruit is thick skinned, sweet and refined ni flavor; the "Plant vert doré," whose thin-skinned and juicy berries yield a less generous wine; and the "Plant gris," which is grown largely at Verzenay and Verzey, and from whose brownish fruit a light perfumed wine is produced. The fourth is the "Chardonnay," which is grown around Côte d'Avize. This fruit produces fine, round, transparent, golden grapes and a delicate, elegant wine.

Since champagne is almost always a blend of several or more wines from various vineyards, and since some are made from black (Pinot Noir) grapes and some from white (Chardonnay) grapes, the most important thing to know about champagne is the reputation of the blender or shipper whose name appears on the label as a guide to quality. After all, it is his ability, proven by the quality of wines he has shipped over a period of years, that counts. The blends of each shipper are closely guarded secrets of the house, so that particular blends or cuvées of certain shippers become well known for a high grade of quality champagne. A reliable shipper will not bottle wine of a poor vintage year, but will blend a quantity of fine wine with it and bottle the blend as a nonvintage wine. This wine, although a nonvintage product, will be superior to a vintage wine of a poor year. The finest champagnes produced by the leading shippers will be crops of fine vintage years and will be labeled Brut or Nature. The best wines will take between ten and fifteen years in preparing for market, although a wine is really ready for market from five to seven years after the time of vintage.

In the Champagne district, the vintagers are recruited in part locally, but many come from northern and eastern departments. Many of these have as much as thirty to forty years experience behind them. The grapes are picked each fall and after being carefully gathered and deposited in baskets, are transferred to wicker sieves. Women then prune away all doubtful stalks and pick off all bruised or unripe berries. Next the fruit is removed to the pressing house, where as a rule three powerful presses will be found installed, each accommodating more than four tons of grapes, which give on an average of fifteen casks of wine, ten being the product of the first pressing or cuvée, while the remainder is of inferior quality.

The must, as the newly expressed wine is called, is transferred to large vats, where it remains for a few hours until it has deposited its mucous lees, whereupon it is drawn off into casks and removed to the cellars where the first fermentation takes place. Towards the end of the year samples are drawn and carefully tasted, the cuvées then being constituted, and the necessary blending takes place in gigantic tuns or vats. The aim of this blending is to combine and develop the special qualities of the respective growths.

In the spring, before the sap begins to run in the vines, the wine will be ready for bottling. The bottling also hinges on the judgment of the cellar master. As soon as he feels that the cuvée has reached the pitch of perfection, the wines are ready for bottling. The next operation is the washing of the bottles. First the bottles are placed over the mouth of a pipe and a jet of sand and water is forced into them, the pressure being so great that the jet will shoot thirty feet high, if the bottle is removed before the pressure is turned off. Then each bottle is cleaned by an equally powerful jet of water. When they are drained, the bottles are ready to be filled. The glass used in the construction of the bottles is very strong and the composition of the glass is strictly regulated. Each bottle is tested before being used for bottling.

The bottles are then filled under elaborate bottling machinery and the contents secured with corks stout enough to resist the pressure caused by fermentation. This cork wood comes principally from Catalonia, Spain. After the corks have been driven into the bottle, they are secured with metal clips. The bottles are then stacked on trucks and carted away to be lowered into the cellars.

In the cellars the wine is stacked to a height of six feet, twenty bottles being placed one above the other. When the fermenation is well over in November the bottles are removed to another cellar to ascertain if any breakage or leakage has occurred during the interval. Such losses rarely exceed 1 per cent. After about three more years the bottles are placed, neck downward and slantwise, in racks standing about six feet high. The object of this is to dislodge any sediment in the wine from the sides of the bottles and collect it on the corks and this is hastened by a workman who, with a quick mechanical turn of the wrist, shakes the bottles daily. However, this process takes about three to four months before the wine is perfectly clear. Then the bottles are removed from the rack and stacked perpendicularly head downwards, pending the so-called operation of disgorging.

When all of the sediment has been precipitated on the cork, the neck of the bottle is inserted into a refrigerating unit which freezes a crust of ice over the sediment in the neck. The bottles are then passed to the disgorger, who unloosens the clip securing the cork, which at once flies out, carrying with it the sediment imprisoned in the ice. The neck of the bottle is then carefully cleaned and the wine tested for clearness or other defect. If the wine is perfect, a temporary cork is inserted.

If the wine is to be shipped Brut (that is, in the perfectly dry natural state) no liqueur or sweetening is added. However, if the wine is to be of a sweeter variety, a little wine is drawn out of each bottle by means of a syphon and a certain predetermined amount of the liqueur (made from still champagne and sugar candy) is added. Finally, the last cork is inserted and securely wired to the neck of the bottle.

The preparation of the wine is now complete and the bottles are stacked in the cellars again for a period of about five months to rest and further marry the wine. The wine is then ready for packing and shipping and taken to the packing department, where the bottles are decorated with silver foil, cravatted, labeled, swathed in pink tissue-paper and cloaked in a straw jacket before being placed in wooden cases.

The following is a list of most of the finest houses producing Champagne: Bollinger, Lanson Père Et Fils, Louis Roederer, Perrier Jouet, Paul Ruinart & Co., Ayala, Ernest Irroy, Montebello, Salon, G. H. Mumm & Co., Moet & Chandon, Veuve Cliquot, Pol Roger, Pommery & Greno, Heidsieck Monopole, Piper Heidsieck, Charles Heidsieck, Delbeck, Binet, Geissler, Goulet, Lemoine, Duetz, Krug & Co., and Bouche Fils.

Champagne is also graded according to sweetness. The amount of liqueur added depends upon the market to which the wine is being shipped and the excellence of the wine itself. The sweeter wines are usually sent to the Continental European markets, while the Bruts or drier wines are shipped to England or the United States. The finest wines have little or no sugar added. The French designations on the bottle as to the amount of sugar that has been added and the average sweetness of the wine are as follows:

Nature	Contains no added sweetening
Brut	Contains up to 1% sweetening
Extra Dry	Contains up to 3% sweetening
Sec or Dry	Contains up to 5% sweetening
Demi-Sec	Contains up to 8% sweetening
Demi-Doux	Contains up to 10% sweetening
Doux	Contains up to 12% sweetening

French Burgundy

Burgundy has long been considered the wine of kings and at the present time many a lover of fine wines has pledged his allegiance to the wines grown in the Province of Burgundy. The generous vinous growths of Burgundy have always been in high regard and centuries ago wines and vines alike of this favored province passed as presents from one royal personage to another.

The "Côte d'Or" or "Golden Slope," for purposes of classifying the products, can be divided into the Côte de Nuits and the Côte de Beaune, the former boasting some of the most esteemed Burgundies produced. The whole district itself is none too large, being about thirty-five miles long and about a mile wide. In fact, the whole district is no larger than one single claret-producing commune of the Médoc district.

In the Côte de Nuits, the finest burgundies are located around the town of Vosne and are known as the Romanée Conti, Richebourg, Romanée St. Vivant, La Tâche and a few others. Of these, Romanée Conti is recognized as king. The characteristics of this splendid wine are body combined with extreme finesse, velvety softness, rich ruby color and a delicate bouquet. Genuine Romanée Conti is rarely met, since the whole vintage rarely exceeds 4,000 bottles.

Richebourg and La Tâche are equally fine wines along with Romanée Conti and the latter has the merit of being a stout wine, all the component parts of which are intimately mingled. Moreover, a wine of this character can form a deposit without becoming thin. Ordinarily, even moderate development wears out the best Burgundies, so that a younger wine of the same quality and a superior vintage may be found superior to an older vintaged Burgundy. The Burgundies of the Côte de Nuits are outstanding because of their vigor, strength, great fullness, and the ability to improve with age — characteristics which most of the wines of the Côte de Beaune do not have.

Clos de Vougeot is usually classed after Richebourg, although connoisseurs generally give the palm to Chambertin, which is a finer type of Volnay. Chambertin has considerable body along with fine flavor, a suave bouquet, great finesse, and the much prized merit of not becoming thin after a period as the majority of the Burgundy growths do.

Clos de Vougeot has a much more decided and characteristic bouquet than Chambertin. It is likewise a firm wine less refined in flavor, having a slight bitterness, such as exists in Médoc growths when young, which is due to the tannic acid it contains. On this account the wine must remain in wood for about four years.

Among the more spirituous growths distinguished by remarkable body and flavor, but deficient in refinement and bouquet, prominence must be given to St. Georges, a highly generous, robust, even harsh wine which tones down with age without losing substance.

The grand wines of Volnay are firm and delicate, with a distinctive and refreshing flavor slightly suggestive of the raspberry and a seductive bouquet unrivaled by any of the other growths of the Côte d'Or.

Aloxe Corton wines have a full, fine flavor and more bouquet than any other growth of the Côte de Beaune, Volnay excepted. Corton takes equal rank with Volnay and sometimes above, owing to its greater richness and its quality of outliving its less robust rivals. When at ten years of age these are usually becoming dry, thin and withered, Corton will still preserve all the qualities of a grand wine.

The Côte de Beaune wines are inclined to be lighter, more suave, and develop much more quickly. This district, however, produces several very fine wines, among which are: Le Montrachet, Meursault, Corton, Pommard, Volnay, and Côte de Beaune. The first two, though they are white wines, are among the finest white wines produced in the world. The Pommard wines are usually well rounded but are inclined to be dull and heavy although some are quite robust.

The wines from Mâcon and Beaujolais of any repute, both red and white, can be counted on the fingers. There are several good Mâcon wines and a single distinguished one. Beaujolais wines are light and agreeable but occupy an inferior rank. Even the fine Mâcon wines require very special conditions to merit even an approach to the character of fine wines. Having no special high vinous qualities, they are ordinarily at their best as early as their third or fourth year.

Burgundy wines are, as a group, one of the rarest and finest of wines and are therefore much imitated. Almost every country in the world has a wine which it dubs a Burgundy. People are definitely misled when comparing those wines with the wines of the Côte d'Or.

The genuine Burgundies are robust, as virile in their appeal as clarets but also delicate and feminine. At their best there are only several wines which equal them and they are surpassed by none. They really rank among the aristocrats of the wine world.

The finest Burgundies are made from the Pinot (white or black) grape which also produces champagne. The other grape grown in the Burgundy district is the Gammay. This grape in other districts produces credible wines, but in the Côte d'Or produces only vin ordinaire. The Gammay usually produces two to three times as much wine per acre and is much more hardy than the Pinot, but the qualities are far apart.

Many of the Pommards and Chambertins sold today are made of the Pinot grape. These fine authentic Burgundies, while rarer and more expensive, are really worth the trouble. In this case the shipper, the vineyard, and the type of wine are more important when purchasing a Burgundy. Most Burgundies are blended and bottled by shippers who wish to put out a wine of consistent quality. Thus the integrity and reputation of this shipper becomes of prime importance since two bottles of Chambertin of the same vintage shipped by two different firms may be as different as day from night.

Winegrowing in this district is different from that in the Bordeaux. In Burgundy, the vineyards are owned by large numbers of small proprietors who grow and prepare the wine. An example of this is in the Clos de Vougeot. This entire vineyard has roughly 127 acres and is owned in part by 52 different shippers. This is an average of less than 3 acres per shipper. After the wine has been prepared, the wine merchants purchase the output of a number of the small proprietors for blending and bottling under the shipper's own label. This blending permits the shipper to market a product of uniform quality every year.

The most famous of the named Burgundies are:

Red Wines

Chambertin, Clos de Vougeot, Clos de Beze, Les Grand Eschezeaux, Romanée Conti, La Romanée La Tâche, Richebourg, Romanée St. Vivant, Saint Georges, Les Fèves, Les Grèves, Clos de Roi, Cailles Le Corton.

White Wines

Le Montrachet, Chablis Moutonne, Meursault Peinère, Chablis Valmar, Meursault Charmes, Le Chevalier Montrachet, Chassagne Montrachet.

The District wines most commonly met are:

Volnay, Beaune, Pommard, Mâçon, Beaujolais, Nuit St. Georges, Gevry Chambertin, Chablis, Pouilly.

The heavy red Burgundies are excellent when served with roasts or wild game. The white wines are ideal with fish of all kinds and with shellfish. Chablis alone is excellent when served with oysters or clams.

The wines of Burgundy vary from year to year much more than the wines of Bordeaux. Only about half of the vintage years actually turn out wines of fine calibre and which can be termed vintage wines.

White Burgundies

Chassagne enjoys with Puligny the honor of producing the finest white wine of the Côte d'Or, namely Le Montrachet. This wine is to the Côte d'Or white Burgundies what Château d'Yquem is to Sauternes and Johannisberger is to the Rhine wines. Native Burgundians maintain that Montrachet is the grandest white wine in the world. The distinguishing characteristics of this fine wine are finesse, fullness, absolute homogeneity and softness combined with a powerful yet delicate flavor and immense richness.

It has, moreover, a most characteristic and eminently suave bouquet very distinctly developed and will keep almost any length of time without losing a single one of its excellent characteristics or qualities. Genuine Le Montrachet commands a high price although the Chevalier and the Batard qualities, the former made from vines at the summit of the hill and the latter at the base, are less expensive but lack the finer qualities.

Meursault wines are firm, soft wines with a fragrant, vivacious flavor. Age usually renders these wines thin and weak, but when well preserved they develop a fragrant vinous dryness.

The village of Chablis lies about 60 miles northwest of the Côte d'Or. Surrounding the village are about 1,000 acres of gently sloping vineyards, in a district known as the district of the Yonne. This wine is thin, pale and delicate and with the distinguishing flinty taste which is the recognized characteristic of these wines. These wines are produced from the Pinot grape and are of a pale golden color.

Pouilly is a fine wine and can be the peer of all but the very finest Chablis. It is very pale, with delicate color, and is usually a little sharp and hard when young, but after about seven to eight years it develops into an extraordinary combination of dryness and subtle richness.

French Bordeaux Clarets

France has been termed the "vineyard of the earth." Not only does France produce more wines but it produces more fine wines than any other country in the world. Of all of the wines not made in France only Port, Sherry, Tokay, Madeira, Rhine and Moselle can be ranked as peers of the great vintages of France. All other wine-producing countries — Germany, Spain, Hungary, and Portugal — combined can offer no such range and variety as is offered by a national collection such as claret, sauternes, burgundy, and champagne.

Not all of the wines produced in France are good; in fact, more than half of them are poor. These wines lacking in any quality whatsoever are sold at several francs per bottle and are called *vins ordinaires* by the French people. The country of France consumes much more wine than she produces and in order to overcome the shortage, the finer vintages are sold in international trade while cheap wines are imported from Algeria and other wine-producing districts.

Bordeaux produces considerably more fine wines than any other wine district in Europe. This tranquil region, undisturbed by torrid world trade, was famous for its wines even in the days of Caesar and Nero. At its finest quality, Bordeaux wine is a long-lived wine of great suavity and grace, balanced, rich and delicate as only a great wine can be, fit for the tables of kings and the altars of the gods. Even at its worst Bordeaux wine is a delightful, sound *vin ordinaire*.

The Bordeaux District produces an astonishing variety of wines: Graves, fresh and clean from the vineyards of Leognan and Pessac; majestic, golden sauternes, almost overpowering in the depth and strength of their bouquet; great clarets which acknowledge no superiors and few equals among the red wines of the world. The appellation *claret* applies to wines produced in the department of the Gironde whose main city is Bordeaux. Therefore, while claret is a distinct type of wine, it has a definite geographical origin in Bordeaux.

Of all the wines of France, Bordeaux are least often tampered with and blended. Unlike most all other French wines, they offer the greatest measure of authenticity and quality. This is due to the practice of château bottling and the precise manner in which the Bordeaux district is divided and classified. The classification and divisions are very complex to the average wine-drinking layman but château-bottled wines and district wines are of two different qualities and thus the layman can soon buy and drink the wines of Bordeaux intelligently. The name *Bordeaux* alone on a bottle does not guarantee quality but origin only, since inferior wines are also produced in this district.

Bordeaux is divided by law into eight districts: three of these — Côtes, Entre Deux Mers, and Palas — produce little except *vin ordinaire*. The other five are of great importance.

Médoc, northwest of Bordeaux, is the home of most of the great clarets; Graves produces several great clarets and numerous excellent dry white wines; Sauternes, bounding Graves on the south, produces white dessert wines exclusively; St. Emelion and Pomerol, east of Bordeaux, are, like Médoc, districts producing red wines but wines generally fuller and less fine than that of Médoc. These five districts are then divided into communes or townships. Naturally some of these communes even in this great district produce better wines than others. Thus Pauillac in the Médoc is superior to St. Laurant. In the following list of some of the communes producing at least some fine wines are put down in order of their importance and in which district of Bordeaux they belong:

Médoc	*Graves*	*Sauternes*
Pauillac	Pessac	Sauternes
Margaux	Léognan	Bommes
Cantenac	Martillac	Preignac
St. Julien	Tallence	Barsac
St. Estephe	Cadujac	Fargues
St. Laurant		
Maçau		

St. Emelion	*Pomerol*
St. Emelion	Pomerol
St. Christophe	
St. Laurant des Combes	

The wines even in a commune are not consistent in quality, since each vineyard may have different slopes of drainage. Some areas there fore will be favored and only great wines will be produced in these favored vineyards. These acres invariably belong to châteaux with established names and proud prosperous owners. The finest wines of a commune do not bear the name of the commune always, but the name of the châteaux around which they are produced. Thus a Château Latour sold as a Château Latour is really a Pauillac, a Médoc and a Bordeaux wine as well.

Of over 200 châteaux in the Bordeaux district producing fine wines, one-third are in the Médoc. The official classification was created in 1855 by a special commission appointed to judge and divide the Bordeaux into categories of the outstanding châteaux of the Médoc and Sauternes. This list sets forth a true appraisal of the various qualities of the famous Médoc wines. The châteaux were then divided into five categories. Only 3 were accorded the highest rank — Château Margaux, Château Lafite Rothschild, and Château Latour. Sixteen were placed in the second class, 14 in the third class, 11 in the fourth class, and 17 in the fifth class.

Below these rankings, although producing excellent wines, are châteaux not in the noble class. Very few of these common château bottlings are sold in America. Since 1855, changes in wines have been noted, since some of the châteaux may have been more scrupulously cared for than others. Therefore certain wines are better than they were seventy-five year ago and certain wines less good. Château Mouton Rothschild, generally recognized as the best of the second growths, very often brings higher prices than Latour or Margaux. However, despite several exceptions, the original classification still holds valid.

The lower-classed châteaux produce wines, in a good year, easily the equal of any natural red wine produced, outside of France, in the world. The higher-classed vineyards were so placed because of their ability to produce wines, in bad years as well as good, which are more or less distinguished; secondly, because of their ability to produce wines which are long lived and improve with time; third, because, under favorable conditions and in a good year, they yield wines which possess, to a supreme degree, the qualities characteristic of all Médoc wines, the unmistakable bouquet, the smoothness, the balance, and finesse.

No effort was made in 1855 to classify the Graves district although it was impossible to ignore Château Haut Brion. This great red wine was placed on a par with the *premier grand crus,* Latour, Margaux, and Lafite Rothschild. Other Graves red wines ranking with the second or third class in the Médoc are Château La Mission Haut Brion, Latour Haut Brion, Pape Clément and Haut Gardère. These share the surpassing qualities of Château Haut Brion but are generally fuller in body and longer lived than corresponding wines of the Médoc. They lack, if anything, the smoothness and finish of the great Médoc clarets.

Château Lafite Rothschild is famous for its magnificent color, exquisite softness, delicate flavor, and fragrant bouquet. Château

Haut Brion is not as delicate and fragrant but has splendid color and more body. This château was once owned by Tallyrand.

Château Margaux (Médoc) in good years has certainly no superior and scarcely an equal. It is a wine generous without potency; it boasts of a bouquet that clings to the lips and perfumes the breath.

The fourth *premier cru* is Château Latour, which derives its name from a massive, ancient, round tower which in history the English assailed and defended by turn during the wars in Guienne. It is a wine distinguished from Château Margaux and Lafite by greater alcohol content, a more pronounced flavor, and a more powerful bouquet which has been compared to the odor of almonds and noyaux combined.

The seductive bouquet common to all the grand wines of the Gironde is understood to be due to an extremely volatile oil, the elements of which are contained in the skins of the grapes, and it requires time for its development. Particular conditions, met with only in certain soils, temperatures and aspects, are requisite to the formation of this perfume, which rarely exists in wines of a generous character, either because the odor of the alcohol conceals it or because the long fermentation necessary to decompose all the various principles causes it to disappear completely.

St. Julien has as one of its first growth wines Guraud Larose Sarget. This wine, like most of the higher class St. Juliens, has a deeper color and greater body and vinosity than the more delicate products of Latour and Lafite. Its bouquet closely resembles the raspberry. This wine must be kept in wood for several years to develop all the qualities of a grand wine.

With but one single exception all the grand wines of the Gironde are produced in the celebrated Médoc district within the space of some twenty miles and along a strip of undulating ground, narrow in size but boundless in renown, bordering the Garonne, a principal river.

The marked superiority of the Médoc wines, which rendered them famous throughout the world, is due to the loose, gravelly and flinty soil and its Ferrueginous ingredients — the presence of 9 per cent of iron having been ascertained by analysis. It has been remarked that whenever wine of superior quality is produced, the soil, no matter what its composition may be, is invariably found to be mixed with fragments of rock in a greater or lesser degree and of varied shapes and sizes. The rounded and light-colored pebbles with which the soil of the Médoc is strewn act as so many reflecting agents, directing the solar rays upward, which concentrate the full power of the sun on the grapes and bathe them in a continual flood of light and heat. These pebbles, too, by reason of their particular composition, have the quality of retaining the heat imparted to them long after the sun has sunk to rest.

There are several admirable Bordeaux wines which have never been château bottled (bottled in the château around which they are produced). These wines are not marked with the familiar phrase, "Mis en bouteille au Château." The purchaser of wine, therefore, does not have definite knowledge concerning these wines and should firmly entrench himself behind the "Mis du Château." A wine which is château bottled is always genuine. Wines, château bottled, have branded corks and labels which give notice to the effect that it is château bottled.

Usually no château-bottled claret (or sauternes) is fit to drink before it has reached five years of age. After a great vintage, they reach full development after ten to twelve years of age and improve for ten to tweny more years afterwards. In poor vintages, the wines should be drunk before the seventh to eighth birthday.

White Bordeaux

White wines that stand on equal footing with the great clarets are found in the Sauternes district of the Bordeaux. This section is to the white wines of Bordeaux what the Médoc is to the red. Each rolling hill has its famous château and each village its famous vineyard.

Sauternes are medium sweet wines, in fact too sweet to drink much of, except as a dinner wine served with the dessert. Sauternes are, along with the great Tokays, the Throckenbeerenauslese of the Rhine, incomparably the best natural sweet wines in the world — rich, full, and possessed of a bouquet as superb as it is inimitable. In general, Sauternes are the most expensive nonsparkling wines made in France, not because of limited supply, but because of the very low yield per acre of vineyard since the grapes are left on the vine until they are over-ripe and covered with a noble-mould.

The two white wines of the Gironde most highly regarded are the renowned Château d'Yquem of the Marquis de Lur Saluces and Château Latour Blanche. Château d'Yquem is the most luscious and delicately aromatic of wines. For its resplendent color resembling liquid gold, its exquisite bouquet and rich delicious flavor due, according to chemists, to the presence of Mannite, it is regarded in France as unique. Mannite has the peculiar quality of not becoming transformed into alcohol and carbonic acid during the process of fermentation. The other first-ranking white wine of France, Château Latour Blanche, is rated immediately below Château d'Yquem. It is a magnificent liqueur-like sauternes though not as sweet as Château d'Yquem.

The characteristic qualities of Château d'Yquem are due to no simple accident. On the contrary, the vintaging of this wine is an extremely complicated and delicate affair. In order to insure the excessive softness and rich liqueur character which are its distinguishing qualities, the grapes, naturally excessively sweet and juicy, are allowed to dry on their stalks, preserved by the rays of the sun, until they become covered with a kind of down which gives an almost mouldy appearance. During this period the fruit, under the influence of the sun, ferments within its skin, thereby attaining the requisite degree of ripeness akin to rot.

On the occasion of the vintage, since it is essential that the grapes be gathered when perfectly dry and warm, the cutters do not commence until the sun has reached a certain height and suspend their operations only when rain threatens or mists begin to form. At the first gathering they detach only the grapes which have dried after reaching proper maturity, the rest being neglected. From the former, a wine of extreme softness and density, termed "Crème de Tête," is produced. After the first gathering is completed, the other grapes will have sufficiently ripened and rotted or dried.

Both sorts are now detached, yielding the wine called "Vin de Tête," distinguished by equal softness with the Crème de Tête, but combined with greater alcoholicity and greater delicacy of flavor. By the end of October, after the remaining grapes have matured, the third gathering produces a wine called the "center," frequently fine and spiritous. Then the final gathering, in which all the grapes remaining on the stalks are picked, produces a wine called the "de Queue" or the "ends."

The juice is then extracted by means of an ordinary wine press and the must is at once put into casks where it is left to ferment for three weeks to a month, during which time it throws off whatever impurities it contains.

The Sauternes district is comprised of five communes: Barsac, Preignac, Bommes, Sauternes, and Fargues. Barsac is the only one of these communes whose wines will bear its own name rather than the generic name of Sauternes.

Barsac

Barsac almost always displays equal finesse with the higher-class
sauternes, combined with greater body, perfect dryness, a more
powerful perfume, and the generous warmth in which the sauternes
is altogether deficient. The majority of Barsacs have a flinty flavor
characteristic because of the abundant amount of salts and iron and
the calcareous nature of the subsoil in which the vines are planted.

Most of the French sweet white wines are sulphured so as to
arrest their fermentation and prevent the whole of the sugar from
becoming converted into alcohol. The use of sulphur has not been
regarded as a disadvantage to the wine, if the fermentation has been
completely stopped and the sulphur consequently removed by popular tapping.

The Graves district lies immediately south of the city of Bordeaux and also produces some very palatable dinner wines. The
district gets its name from the gravelly quality of the soil and produces more red wine than white. The white wines are sold under the
name of Graves and Graves Supérieurs. The red Graves are, taken
as a whole, better than the white; the latter, if rarely great, are among
the most pleasant of table wines, fresh, clean, balanced, and reason-
ably dry.

There are a great number of famous châteaux in the Graves
district, some producing claret and some white wines. Château
Olivier and Château Carbonnieu are perhaps the best known growths
producing white wines. Several communes in the Graves produce
excellent dessert wines very much like sauternes.

The Sauternes district was, like the Médoc, classified in 1855
and Château d'Yquem, alone, ranked as a *premier grand cru* (great
first growth) and eleven others as *premier crus* (first growths). The
white wines are rigidly classed into three groups of which Château
d'Yquem is the *unique premier cru*. The classified wines form 2 per
cent of the total production, superior table wines about 12 per cent,
the medium quality wines about 20 per cent and the *vins ordinaires*
about 66 per cent.

There are many more châteaux in the Sauternes district that
produce white wines than in the Graves. The most famous of these
are: Château d'Yquem, Château Latour Blanche, Château Guiraud,
and Château Climens. All of these châteaux practice what is known
as *château bottling.* Under this practice the wines grown on the vineyards of each proprietor and each individual château are developed,
bottled, and labeled by the proprietor of each château. The wines
which are of the finest quality are identified by the French phrase, on

the label, cap, and cork, "Mis en bouteille au Château." This inscription is a guiding phrase that the wines were grown, developed and bottled by the proprietor of the château.

French Wines of the Rhône Valley

The most famous wines of the Côte d'Or Rhône are the red, white, and straw-colored Hermitage and the Château-Neuf-du-Pape. The Hermitage wines have a remarkable clean, fresh, full, vinous flavor combined with a softness and are of a rich, deep purple hue.

The white Hermitage of a pale yellow tint and with an ambrosial perfume that may be pronounced unique, is exquisitely suave, rich and spiritous in flavor and perfectly dry. The straw-colored Hermitage is a vinous, luscious, almost unctuous wine, having volume, richness, delicious smoothness, combined with refreshing sharpness free from the slightest acidity.

Chateau-Neuf-du-Pape is an intensely deep-colored wine of great volume and with a particular sweet, bitterish taste. This wine was once the daily beverage of the Avignon popes.

The Côtes du Rhône vineyards are just south of Burgundy toward the Mediterranean where the olive trees begin. The wines are rich in alcohol and tannin, rough and powerful when young. The red Rhône wines are deeper in color than the Burgundies. The white wines, hiding behind a splendid bouquet, have an unsuspected strength. The wines of this district throw a deposit and have to be decanted with great care before serving. The vineyards of the Rhône district have been defined by law and are quite reliable.

French Vouvray

Vouvray, near the city of Tours, produces a wine second only to that of the Anjou among the vintages of the Loire. This wine, called Vouvray, is light, fresh, fragile, pale, and at its best only in the finer qualities which have the body, strength and tannic content that are the guarantees of an ability to improve with time. Vouvray, of the white variety, is the produce of the large and small white Pineau vines, the latter being the best bearer and yielding the finer and sweeter fruit.

Still white Vouvray in good years and from a vineyard with a favorable reputation, and above all when made with proper care, attains a degree of perfection which raises it almost to the first rank among the finest white wines. The taste is very pleasant and fragrant, but its keeping and traveling powers vary. Because of the large amount of sugar content in the wine, it undergoes several stages or changes during the process of development. While passing through these stages, the great sweetness subsides and a quantity of carbonic acid gas is developed. The presence of this gas in the wine gives it an effervescent, live taste not unlike a very mildly sparkling wine. When the wine emerges from this latter stage, it generally loses its liqueur-like flavor and becomes very potent.

Vouvray of a great year will keep for many years, as long as forty to fifty, and still retain the fine, high flavor. It has been said that Vouvray will not travel well, but that statement is erroneous since the wine has been tested in this country after an ocean voyage and found to be as good as when it left Vouvray.

A sparkling Vouvray is also produced in this district and is much like champagne, only a bit sweeter. This wine is very fine but as yet has not been greatly publicized.

Since the Vouvray wines are petulant or mildly effervescent, a very hard cork is used. This cork is then securely wired by means of a clip to the top of the bottle so that the internal pressure will not blow out the cork while the wine is traveling and also to keep the wine from losing the live qualities that distinguish it from almost all the other wines of France.

French Alsatian Rhine Wine

French Rhine wines, as the Alsatian wines are called are good and some of them are excellent, but they can no more rival a Schloss Johannisberg than they can authentic Montrachet. When the province was in the hands of Germany, little attention was paid to the wines of this district, but after the French came into possession good care was shown to these wines. Since the war, they have exploited them much more than they have ever been before.

Despite the excellent care the French have given these wines, they will never be the peers of the finest German Rhine wines. They do, however, resemble the Rhine wines more than they do the French wines. The District of Alsace is the southernmost district of the Rhine vineyard region.

The Alsatian Rhine wines for the most part are pleasant, clean, dry, and possessed of an admirable, delicate flavor and bouquet.

Most of these wines are produced from the Riesling grape, which ranks with the Pinot and Chardonnay. The other wines of this district are named after the vines from which they are produced, such as Riesling, Traminer, Tokay, Sylvaner and several others.

German Wines

The Rhine and Moselle vineyards are the most northerly in the world. Consequently great care and scientific culture are necessary to produce the fine wines for which this district is noted. The wines are more hardy and dry than the French wines, since they must develop and ripen in a very short space of time. Although Germany produces and consumes a very small percentage of the wine that France does, German wines rank almost on a par with the French wines. In fact, on the average, the wines of Germany have finer quality than any country in the world. Most of the wines of Germany have common characteristics, so that comparisons in their relative merits are much easier than with the varied growths of Bordeaux and Burgundy.

Most of the wines originate with the Riesling vine, which predominates among all the grapes produced in the Rhine and Moselle districts. This vine alone is responsible for the common characteristics which most Rhine and Moselle wines have — those of delicate bouquet, fine flavor, greater richness that never cloys, lightness that is almost never too thin, clean, refreshing taste, and quality. The Sylvaner grape produces wines that are heavier and less delicate than the Riesling. These wines are found in the Hessian and Pfalz districts.

Rhine wines in the majority, if extremely old, lose their fine, high flavor, nearly all of their fragrant aroma, and retaining only their brilliant color.

A Rhine wine is never fortified with Spirit — in fact, this act even to the humblest *Winzer* of the Rhine country would be a sin which nothing could atone for.

Although the flavor and bouquet of the grand wines of the Rhiengau are equally pronounced, it is exceedingly difficult to characterize all of them with precision. After gratifying the sense of smell with the fragrant perfume which they evolve and which is no mere essence, vanishing as soon as recognized, but often a rich odor which almost scents the surrounding atmosphere, one proceeds to taste the wine and seems to sip the aroma exhaled by it. Now and then there is consciousness of a refined pungent flavor and at other times of a slight racy sharpness, while the flavor and aftertaste generally suggest more of an almond flavor than any other wine. No wines vary so much in their finer qualities as the grand growths of the Rheingau. The produce of one particular vineyard, although from the same species of grape cultivated under precise similar conditions, will differ materially in flavor and bouquet, not only in bad or good years, but also in excellent vintages. These wines, moreover, need very skillful cellar treatment during the long years they are developing. All great wines ripen slowly and cannot be quickly developed by heating as ordinary wines may be.

There are no purer nor better white wines in the world than the fine growths of the Rhine. Excepting in the case of the sweet Ausleses, they are always perfectly fermented, but unfortunately, their higher qualities are entirely dependent on the perfect ripening of the grapes which, as may be supposed in so northern a latitude, is a matter of considerable uncertainty.

When the vintage is good, the wine growers have to recoup themselves of their losses suffered in bad years, when the wine, exceedingly acid, fetches a mere percentage of its ordinary price. Moreover, Rhine wines require several years to develop themselves, during which interval they are the object of unceasing attention. It naturally follows, therefore, that the normal price of the best Rhine growths rates high, far higher, indeed, in proper proportion than the premier growths of the Médoc command. Again mere rarity alone in the case of the superior growths causes these to attain a purely fantastic figure which year after year exhibits an increase as Germany grows richer, for most of the grand Rhine wines are consumed at home.

Steinberger Wine

Steinberger, a really outstanding Rhine wine, is made only from the over-ripe grapes in the same manner as the Schloss Johannisberg. The Schloss Johannisberg vineyard is owned by Prince Von Metêrnich. This great wine has on each cork and label the imprint of the Prince's crest, which corresponds to the château designation of estate-bottled clarets and sauternes.

Oestricher Auslese is made from the most perfect, ripest grapes grown, and, moreover, under the very best conditions. Another very fine wine is the Marcobrünner which gets its name from the river of the same name. This river rises a little distance from the Rhine, and works its way through the Marcobrünner Vineyard. The whole vineyard produces only 8,000 to 10,000 bottles yearly and only 20 per cent of this total is bottled as Marcobrünner.

In all four districts — that is, in the Moselle, Rheingau, Rheinhessen, and the Rheinpfalz, the labeling terminology used is uniform. The various designations of the Rhine labels are important to know when attempting to order wines correctly and intelligently. Most of these labels carry information as to the name of the vineyard, and town where the wine was made. Other information includes the vintage year and a designation which tells the amount of sugar in the wine and whether the wine is an Auslese or a Spatlese, etc.

Definitions of Designation of Sweetness or Ripeness

Gezuckerter Wein
Wine which has had sugar added, although the wine may still be dry or sweet.

Naturwein or Ungezuckerter Wein
The grapes used in this wine are ripe but not over-ripe. It is comparatively dry and if made by a good vineyard in a good vintage year will be excellent.

Auslese
This is a wine produced from selected bunches of grapes. This process produces some of the best dry wines made in Germany. They are richer and fuller than the others.

Beerenaulese
This wine is made from individually selected grapes from selected bunches. These grapes are transparent and covered with the noble mould. A wine of this type is full, rich and very expensive, and is only made in exceptional years.

Throckenbeerenauslese
This wine is made from semi-dried grapes, individually selected. The wine is pressed from these grapes which have been dried by the late Autumn sun and are made only once or twice in a decade. Always very expensive, this wine is one of the best and one of the sweetest natural wines to be had.

Spatlese
These grapes are allowed to hang on the vine until they are partially dry and covered with the noble mould. This wine is very fine, sweet, rich in alcohol, and quite expensive.

Edelbeeren
This phrase also denotes a wine made from grapes which have been allowed to become over-ripe.

Cabinet

This word indicates a wine, no matter what the type, of the finest and rarest quality available.

The German wine laws are very stringent and are upheld accordingly. Thus when a wine is described to be of a certain quality, the buyer can rely on that description. When a wine label contains the word — Wachstum-Gewaecks or Originalabfullung, the meaning conveyed is that the wine is estate bottled, that is, that the wine was bottled under the personal supervision of the owner of the vineyard. No sugared wine is ever labeled with any of these words and only the finest of the other vintages are bottled in this manner.

The fine Rhine wines come mainly from four districts: The Rheingau, The Rheinhessen, The Palatinate or Pfalz, and the Moselle. All four of these lie in or around the beautiful Rhine Valley. The various towns and vineyards lend their names to the innumerable vintages of this region and their multiplicity make mistakes in ordering or recongnition very easy. However, there is only a small percentage which the wine drinker really should know.

The Rheingau

The Rheingau district is the finest wine-producing region of Germany and produces white wines which have no peers in the world. These wines on the average do not have the long life of the Bordeaux wines, but in the fine vintages among the *grand vins,* the length of life is materially longer.

The main aim of the vine growers is quality, since there is no great abundance of acreage in the whole of the Rheingau district. In all there are not more than 6,000 acres under vines. The great Rhine wine producing vineyards comprise a total of only about 1,000 acres. Because of this scarcity of acreage in the really fine Rhine wines, the scarcity and often high prices is explained.

Most of the districts lie near the river, while others are several miles away. Of these, the best known are Johannisberger, Rudesheim, Hochheim, and Steinberger. The Schloss Johannisberg and the Steinberger are rated as the two greatest wines of the Rheingau. Almost all of the vines in this district are of the Riesling grape. The above two wines are known as Cabinet wines and belong to a world of pomp and ceremonial which are the only circumstances in which these wines should really be drunk and appreciated. The characteristics of most of the wines of the Rheingau are zestful bouquet and rounded, full taste.

Among the best growths of the Rheingau are:

Rudesheimberg	Erbacher Marcobrünner
Rudesheimer Schlossberg	Eltviller Sonnenberg
Schloss Johannisberg	Hochheimer Daubhaus
Oestricher	Rauenthaler Rothenberg
Steinberger	

The Wines of Rheinhessen

The Hessian wines on the average are full-bodied and quite rich in alcohol, containing as much as 12 to 13 per cent in comparison to the Moselles, which have about 8 to 9 per cent. The finest of these wines are soft, round and generous, but lack the delicacy and liveliness of the Moselles. Finally, they do not possess the distinction that the Great Rheingau have.

In the very old and quaint city of Worms lies the most famous single vineyard of the Rheinhessen — that known as Leibfrauenstift. This small vineyard is located in a city churchyard and was the original home of the wine now known as Liebfraumilch. This title at the present time does not denote a definite origin, but simply refers to a type of Hessian wine of certain characteristics which is now produced in various vineyards.

The predominant vine produced in this district is the Oestricher or Sylvaner, which produces wines which are very good, but usually lack character and have a very short life in comparison to the other growths of the Rhine Valley. In fact, these wines improve very little with time and very seldom last much longer than twelve to fifteen years.

Some of the most important Hessian vineyards are:

Commune	Vineyard
Nackenheim	Rothenberg, Kahlenberg
Oppenheimer	Sacktrager, Goldberg, Herrenberg
Nierstein	Daubhaus, Domthal, Orbel
Bingen	Rosengarten, Schlossberg
Laubenheimer	
Klostergarten	

The Wines of the Bavarian Palatinate

This district lies due south of Rheinhesse on the left bank of the Rhine, between Hesse and Alsace. The Germans call this section Pfalz, and the wines of this district are quite strong, have more sweetness and less acidity than those of the other Rhine wines. Because of this difference in balance, the wines are inclined to be flat. Unless they are of excellent quality, the Pfalz wines are not as good or as distinguished as the wines of the Rheingau. However, since they are a bit sweeter, they will be as well liked as any of the German wines.

There are over 40,000 acres of vineyards under vines in this district and it is the largest single wine producing area in Germany, producing over 12,000,000 gallons of wine each year. About 80 per cent of this, however, is sold locally in bulk.

There are several different types of grapes grown in this area, namely: Traminer, Riesling, Oestricher, and Gutedel. The climate is very mild and the soil is over-rich to produce the very finest type of wine. Among the best growths of the Pfalz are: Forster Jesueten-garten, Wachenheimer Goldbochel, Durkheimer Spielberg, Diedes-heimer, and Ruppertsberg.

Moselle Wine

Moselle wine derives its name from the River Moselle, which rises in France and flows down to the Rhine at Coblenz. The Moselle vineyards are situated on both sides of the river, and the predominant grapes grown in this district are of the Riesling type.

The small sugar content in the Moselle wines gives them a fragrant, flower-like bouquet and a pleasant dry aftertaste. These wines, though light in body, are long lived and in the finest vintages are rare and very expensive.

The more noted growths of the Moselle are: Piesporter, Braun-berger, Zeltinger, and Berncastler. The latter wine is known as "Bern-castler Doktor" in its finer grades, the most famous of which is pro-duced by the proprietor, Dr. Hugo Thanish, on his estate. The Berncastler wines are inclined to have a slight smoky after-flavor, which is attributed to the slate formations under the vineyards.

The finer vintages of Moselle in the Auslesen type are distin-guished, in spite of their almost too luscious character, by a remark-able fullness of flavor and fragrance of perfume. These wines are very much like a haut sauternes but still have qualities of their own. They will outlast lighter and more delicate wines.

Among the finest growths of the Moselle wines are: Piesporter Goldtropfchen, Graacher Himmelreich, Zeltinger Rotlay, Braun-berger Falkenberg, Berncastler Doktor, Berncastler Schlossberg, Erdener Treoppchen.

The Wines of Austria

The wines of Austria are as diverse as its population. In the extreme south they are so dark and full-bodied that when mixed with an equal quantity of water, they are quite as deep in color and as spiritous as the ordinary wines of Bordeaux. In less favorable districts they are excessively poor and so sour as to rasp the tongue like the roughest cider. Some of the lighter varieties have the delicacy, if not the fragrance, of certain wines of the Rhine district. The fine qualities of the Austrian wines are extremely rare.

Several rather fine wines have been produced in Bohemia and are very much like French Burgundy. This wine is known as Labin. Other varieties of Riesling, Traminer and Sylvaner are of inferior quality, since the care necessary for making fine wines is lacking.

The Wines of Greece

At their best, with moderate development, the Greek wines are unequaled save by certain exceptional, great wines. The red varieties may not have the rare exquisite bouquet and velvety softness of Margaux and Latour, or the roundness of Romanée or Corton, but still they surpass an average Burgundy, besides being more wholesome, and have more genuine vinous flavor than any except the finest natural port wines.

On the island of Crete are made some of the famous Malmseys which have been so well liked in Europe in the past. Mavrodaphne, a very fine wine, has become quite popular in the United States, and is made near Patras. There are also several other sweet wines that are passable, but there are few wines made on the whole that are worth describing in detail.

Australian Wines

The wines of Australia are of a fine character and compare very favorably with the French dry wines. These wines are named after their counterparts in the European vineyards. The Hermitage, Cabernet and Burgundy have the smoothness of the Côte d'Or growths, but not the volume, bouquet, or flavor.

The Cabernet wines are similar to the Médoc wines of France, but are far too thin to carry the extra amount of alcohol they possess which arises from the excess of sugar developed in the grape under the Australian sun. The Australian Riesling and Muscatel also have merit. The wines are of the European type, but in method of production and the qualities achieved closely parallel the wines of California. Most of the wines produced are of the blended type so that a standard of quality is kept.

Italian Wines

The Nation of Italy, with all of her natural advantages, has not yet learned how to produce a really fine dry wine. Aside from the limited number of special growths such as Barolo of Piedmont, the Chianti of Tuscany, the Orvieto and Est! Est!! Est!!! of the Roman States, the Lagrima Christi of Naples, and the Zucco of Cosenza, almost all of her wines lack flavor and bouquet. The Italian wines are invariably rich in color and those of the south are remarkably alcoholic, but these qualities, desirable as they may be, fail to atone for the lack of agreeable taste and aroma. Progress, however, is being made and the wines are continually improving.

About one billion gallons of wine are produced in Italy each year. The acres planted with vines exceed those of France since over 85 per cent of the total area of Italy is under vines. Most of the vines are tended by farmers having little experience and the wines thus suffer from a lack of good care that the French wines receive.

Although improvements are noted in the Italian wines, they are still incompletely fermented, hard to keep, throw an extremely heavy sediment, are very rough, and not sufficiently standardized. Some shippers, however, never sell or ship wines that have any of these faults. Almost all of the exported Italian wines now carry the specific stamp of the government in the form of a National Export Stamp on the neck of each bottle. This stamp does not guarantee that the wine is a very good one or that it is great, only that the wine is pure and authentic.

The finest wines of the northern part of Italy come from the Piedmont Provinces. The most popular of the wines produced there is called Barolo, a red wine much like the finer growths of the Rhône in France. This wine must be kept for at least two years and is at its best after the first decade. Nebiolo and Barbera are inferior growths of the same type of wine. The best wine of this district is the Asti, the sparkling type being called Asti Spumanti. This wine is made in the same manner as champagne but is quite a bit sweeter.

The finest wine of the Province of Tuscany is the red Chianti and the finest vineyard is the Brolio in the vicinity of Sienna. Chianti possesses remarkable finesse and an agreeable subacidity. This wine is not unlike the best Beaujolais growths, with, however, more color, body, and force. The wine is in its prime at its fifth or sixth year, but is drinkable at two to three years of age. It comes packed in a distinctive, straw-covered bottle which is probably more famous than the wine. Chianti also comes in the white variety, which is sweeter, more delicate, and a pale golden color.

In the province of Latium at the town of Orvieto is made the famous wine called Est! Est!! Est!!! This wine is a dry type and sold in the straw covered bottle. It is one of the most pleasant golden wines made in Italy. This district is also renowned for the excellence of its Muscatel.

Lagrima Christi (Tears of Christ) is made on the slopes of Mt. Vesuvius, near the city of Naples. This wine is made in both the red and white varieties from the Greco grapes. The white wine has about 13 per cent alcohol, with a character, bouquet, and flavor all its own. There is also some Lagrima Christi of the sparkling type which is made in the Province of Piedmont. The exceedingly luscious flavor is said to be the result of the loose volcanic soil in which the vines are planted.

The Island of Sicily contributes a very popular wine called Marsala, the most celebrated growth of the island. The finest Marsala is noted for a Madiera-like flavor and great softness. It is only moderately fortified with brandy. The sherry-like flavor and aroma of the Marsala wines is due to the similarity of the soil from which they are produced to that of the Jerez vineyards, both being a compound of carbonate of lime and argil mingled with oxide of iron. Marsala, however, is richer in body, has a highly developed bouquet, a freedom from acidity to taste, and is mellow and oily, in contrast to sherry. This wine in most varieties is fortified with brandy.

A vintage marked on a bottle of Marsala wine refers to the quality of the wine in the blend. Other designations are: S. O. M. — Superior Old Marsala; O. P.—Old Particular; L. P.—London Particular; and O. S.—Old Solera. Much of the Marsala is of the virgin type since it is not fortified with the addition of spirit. This possibility is due to the large amount of sugar in the grape juice and the resultant sufficient amount of alcohol being formed through fermentation to bring the alcoholic content up to the 19 per cent, or at times, more.

Other wines of Sicily include a number of sweet Muscatels and some Malvasia. Both of these are sweet dessert wines and are slightly fortified. The Muscatel of Sicily especially is one of the sweetest of all natural wines.

Italian and French Vermouth

Vermouth is a wine which has had herbs, roots and other flavoring ingredients steeped in it so as to flavor the wine. Although vermouth is made in many parts of the world, the two most important types are the dry French vermouths and the sweet Italian vermouths.

In the process of making the French vermouth, white wines from the choicest vineyards are selected. To these white wines are added the finest spirits to fortify the wine. The blend is allowed to stand in thick oak casks called *demi-muids*. After the wines are thus conditioned for about two years, they are then embodied with the infusions obtained by macerations of numerous special plants in accordance with a duly tested formula. This brings out the characteristic vermouth bouquet.

There are about forty different herbs, plants, roots, leaves, peels, seeds, and flowers used in the process of making French vermouth. Some of these are: nutmeg, coriander seeds, cloves, cinnamon, hyssop, majoram, angelica root, gentian, flowers of elder.

It take about four years to develop and prepare true vermouth properly. This means that enormous reserves must be kept on hand at all times, involving a tremendous investment. Therefore only a few houses produce a really fine product.

French vermouth of a fine quality can be drunk straight as an apéritif for meals. This practice is very popular in France. In the United States, vermouth has its greatest popularity as an ingredient for numerous cocktails.

Italian vermouths are sweet when compared with the French variety. This is due to the fact that the basic wine used for the making of the vermouth is sweeter and fuller than the thin white wines used in making French vermouth. The wine used in making Italian vermouth is called Marsala; in making French vermouth it is called Herault. In addition to this, the herbs used in Italian vermouth are different as are also the seeds, roots, plants, and flowers. A certain amount of bitters is also employed to impart a slight bitter flavor under the sweetness.

Italian vermouth can be developed in a much shorter time than the French. For this reason the reserve stocks do not have to be so large and as a result there are a great many more Italian vermouth houses than there are French. Italian vermouth may be used as an apéritif but its greatest popularity is in the making of cocktails.

Sherry

In the Spanish-speaking countries, the wine we know as sherry is known by the name of a small town, Jerez, from which it comes. The word *sherry* is the English corruption of the manner in which the early London wine merchants pronounced and wrote Jerez. Jerez de La Frontera is in the southern part of Spain, near the city of Cadiz, in the province of Andalusia. This district produces the only genuine sherry in the world. All other wines, though they may be excellent in taste and quality, are not sherry.

The vintage of sherry begins in the early part of September. The grapes are brought to the main building of the vineyards where they are first spread out on straw mats in the courtyard for a few hours in the sun. They are then placed in an oblong pressing trough known as a lager. With special rakes, the grapes are next leveled off into a layer a few inches thick and are sprinkled with a few shovelfuls of chalky earth dust of the vineyard. Another layer of grapes is then raked out and more dust sprinkled over them. This continues until the lager is half full. Men wearing special shoes with pegs protruding from the sides, tread the grapes out thoroughly. This is done to the accompaniment of chanting and singing.

As soon as the treading starts, the juice begins running off through a connecting trough into fresh butts which are casks of about 132-gallon capacity. The butts are only partially filled. As soon as the first fermentation is completed and the wine falls bright, the casks are filled nearly full and are ready to go to the sherry-shippers bodegas in Jerez.

Upon arriving at the bodegas, the newly made wine is left in the courtyard for twelve to eighteen months. During this period the bungs are not driven home, and the wine is allowed to be in direct contact with the air and exposed to the elements. This is done to encourage the flowering of the wine.

The flowering is a special development which is particularly noticed in the production of Amontillado Sherry. A thin film of yeast develops upon the surface of the new wine. This is a secondary fermentation that converts the wine into sherry. Before the flowering, the wine is identical but by the time the flowering is completed, mysterious changes take place in the butt, so that twelve to eighteen months after vintage some of the wine will be found to be the light delicate fino type, some medium in color and taste, some will be golden rich oloroso, and some of the butts may have proven to be a failure, so that the wine can only be used for vinegar.

The wines are classified into three classes: pale dry, medium, and dark sweet wines, and will be transferred into the bodega proper. After another year of expert care, the wines are further classified into definite types and qualities. After two to three years they are placed in the reserve casks. Three or four years later the wine is ready to go into the solera.

Sherry is a blend of several different wines from the Jerez district, each type having a characteristic needed to make the final product complete. The blending is done through a solera. Spanish Solera is created in the following fashion:

A number of butts of a definite type of wine of an exceptionally fine vintage are laid down. A few years later an equal number of butts of the same type of wine are laid down and placed immediately on top of the first tier and a few years later still another tier is placed on top of the second tier. The sherry shipper is then ready to draw wine from the solera for bottling. The amount of wine required for bottling is drawn from the oldest or lowest tier. The butts in this tier are then refilled from the tier immediately above and that in turn from the uppermost tier that contains the youngest wine.

When all of the wine has been drawn off from the uppermost tier, new butts of fresh wine replace the empty casks. In this way there is a constant process of blending going on year after year and thus a definite standard of quality can be maintained for generations.

The different types of sherry shipped from Spain and their descriptions are:

Montilla	Very Pale, and extremely dry
Fino	Pale, dry, light in color and body
Vino De Pasto	Pale, dry, softer than Fino
Amontillado	Vino De Pasto but heavier bodied
Amoroso	Pale, golden, medium
Oloroso	Deep golden, sweet
Solera	Very fine, golden, sweet
Brown	Dark brown, very rich, sweet

Montilla

The Montilla sherry is produced in the Province of Cordova in the walled town of Montilla. The finest wines of this type are produced in the Sierra De Montilla district. These wines develop an Amontillado flavor which develops in the wine when the alcohol absorbs oxygen from the air. This absorption of the atmosphere contributes to the formation alike of the flavor and perfume of the Amontillado. Montilla above all other Spanish wines requires considerable age to arrive at perfection. In the older vintages, the wines are full and mellow with a deeper color than natural sherry, richer in aroma and usually of high splendid flavor.

Vino de Pasto

The Vino de Pasto (table wine) type of sherry is a dry, light, highly flavored sherry. The older Vino de Pasto sherries manifest a fine aroma, and corresponding delicacy, the result invariably of age — a most important element in all Spanish wines of the smallest pretension.

Amontillado

This is an aged Vino de Pasto which has acquired a certain delicacy of bouquet and a darker color. This wine resembles the wines of Montilla. In Spain the popular method of serving this wine is well chilled, as a cocktail before dinner. In the United States this sherry, above all others, has become the most popular.

Oloroso Sherry

The Olorosos are known in their early stages as *palos cortados* since the butts containing them are marked with an upright line intersected with a shorter line intended to indicate a cut stick. These sherries are deeper in color than the Amontillados, have a nutty flavor, and are fuller, richer and mellower to the taste, besides possessing an especially fragrant bouquet. Fine Olorosos develop very well and are inclined to be expensive. This sherry should be used as an after dinner wine.

Fino Sherry

Vino Fino sherries are made from the very finest grapes. After aging they develop into Amontillados and finally into Olorosos. The wines that do not develop remain Vino Fino and are described as pale in color, dry, soft, and delicate in flavor, spiritous yet entirely free from heat and fresh to the taste.

Brown Sherry

The sherries of this class are merely Olorosos of the heaviest type with a very full flavor, dark golden color, nutty taste and full, fragrant bouquet. These wines of the sweeter heavy type are usually made from Raya wine and sweetened with Pedro Ximinex — a very sweet blending wine made from Malaga grapes. This is usually sold as a Solera wine. Another type of brown sherry is the East India kind, which is shipped as ballast to the East Indies and back, since the sherry is improved by the sea voyage.

Manzanilla Sherry

The Manzanilla sherries are thin, dry wines deriving their name from a certain similarity of flavor and fragrance to the Manzanilla or Camomile. These are the purest of all sherries simply because the vintners find that they will not blend well with other growths. This wine is practically colorless, thin in body — with all the natural spirit of the wine suppressed by the bitter medicinal flavor which is a distinguishing characteristic that age does not seem to subdue materially. The soil in the district is composed of clay, sand, and chalk. It is from this peculiarity that the Manzanilla derives its bitter, aromatic flavor. One specialty of this type of sherry is that the must is always perfectly fermented, the result being an exceedingly pale and thin wine entirely free from heat and yet containing a considerable amount of natural alcohol, enabling it to keep for nearly thirty years, and with every year added to its development, sensibly improving in flavor.

A dry sherry, chilled and served as a cocktail preceding dinner, is very popular.

Madeira Wines

The Island of Madeira was discovered in 1418 by John Goncalves Zarco. It was uninhabited by man and very heavily wooded. Its discoverer then set fire to it and the island burned steadily for seven years. The ashes of this fire made the soil exceedingly fertile and later when vines were introduced they prospered wonderfully. Good Madeiras are rare since no great production or quantity is available on this island of only 1,360 square miles.

Madeiras are invariably exported from Funchal. Wines as old as fifty to sixty years in the cask when tested are found to be perfect and do not seem to have passed their prime. These wines, while displaying fullness and vinosity, due partly to the alcohol which was administered when the wine was very young, developed a suppressed bitterness of flavor and emitted a nutty flavor which is characteristic of matured wine.

In order to hasten the development of the wines, they are sent sometimes on voyages to the East or West Indies or subjected to heat and motion by other means. The ultimate desire in either case is to subdue the harsher qualities of the wine.

There is also a type of Madeira rarely seen that is a natural, unfortified wine, free from any adventitious spirit, full, soft, and delicate, but with a distinct, rich, vinous flavor.

The special types of Madeira are:

Sercial	Very dry Madeira—fully matured
Gloria Mundi	Very soft and refined—very little body, color or sugar and yet with much bouquet and power
Old Bual	Luscious sweet wine
Old Malmsey	Deep golden brown, sweet and an excellent dessert wine
Virgin	Unfortified natural wine

Spanish Malaga

Malaga is an extremely sweet slightly fortified, walnut colored wine, containing about 18 per cent alcohol and having a rich, powerful and unmistakable bouquet of Muscat. This liquorous wine is made from the Pedro Ximenes and Muscat grapes, produced in the Granada district of Spain. This is a mountainous district near Malaga that is so favorable for the development of the vine that three crops of grapes are harvested each year.

The dry Malaga wines are made from the second crop, which is gathered in September. The third vintage, gathered in the following months, yields the sweet Malagas. The latter are very rich, deep amber-colored wines in which the bouquet and soft spiritous flavor are the result of age. Malaga has enjoyed the reputation of keeping for a century — perfectly preserved. The older this wine becomes, the drier and more mellow it is.

Malaga is marketed in three types:

1. The first type is the Malaga which is made from the fermented juice of the Pedro Ximenes grapes blended with brandy and boiled with unfermented grape juice called Arrope.

2. The second type of Malaga, the best of all, is known as Lacrima Christi. It is made from the same grapes and in the same manner as Tokay Essence. The grapes are laid in the sun where a thousand pounds of grapes exude from time to time several gallons of precious juice. This juice is then fermented, fortified, and blended with Vino Maestro, a sweet heavy wine made from sun-dried grapes.

3. The third type is called Moscato and is composed of two-thirds Pedro Ximenes and one-third Muscat grapes Vino Maestro, i.e., sweet, half-fermented wine made from Muscat grapes.

Malagas are aged in wood and blended, as with sherry, by the Solera system. They improve with age for over a century and are by far the finest sweet wine produced in Spain.

Portuguese Port Wine

Genuine port wine comes from the Douro Valley, near the city of Oporto in northern Portugal. Portuguese law, in which the English law concurs, has forbidden any wine to be called port unless it comes from the Douro Valley. This section is about thirty-five miles long and ten miles wide.

The country consuming the largest amount of port in the world is England. In fact, port-drinking in England has become somewhat of an institution with much ceremony and ritual accompanying its use. Since the Englishman uses the greater amount of the production of this wine, the blending of grapes is conducted along lines to please his taste.

Port wine, as it is known in England, is at its best a round, heady wine, deep of color with a certain fullness and roundness as its principal merits. Its bouquet, in lieu of the fragrance of fruit or flowers, has too often an odor of ardent spirits. Its most ardent admirers would never claim for it either raciness or freshness of taste. In comparison to other great wines, it is lacking in finesse, those subtle gradations, and that refined harmony of flavor combined with freshness and softness, which distinguish the *grand crus* of the Haut Médoc; added to this, unlike those unique wines, it leaves neither the head cool nor the tongue fresh.

Port wine belongs to the sweet, fortified group of wines. It is rich and robust, fortified with Portuguese brandy during the fermentation. The finer ports from the Douro Valley are characterized by deep color, soft, generous, full body and altogether dry and clean taste, while the less pretentious wines are astringent and spiritous.

Port wine is not just a wine, but necessarily a blend of wines. Mostly as many as fifteen to twenty different wines are used to complete the final product. Because of this fact, there is no single type of grape which is favored — rather a combination of many kinds which separately produce wines of ordinary character, yet when blended turn out port wine of admirable characteristics.

When the grapes are fully ripened, usually during the latter part of September, they are gathered and brought to the pressing house of the vineyard. The grapes are then dumped into a large circular or oblong trough made of stone or cement called a lager. Then to the accompaniment of colorful ceremony and gay music, the grapes are fully trodden until all of the juice has been separated from the stems and skins. The scene is a happy one since those engaged in the work usually sing and dance as they work.

The grapes and the juice called the must are left in the lager to ferment. The must is watched carefully during the fermentation. When precisely the requisite amount of sugar remains unfermented twenty-four to twenty-eight hours later, depending upon the amount of sugar in the must, brandy distilled from the wines of the district and of a previous vintage is added, raising the alcoholic content of the mass up to 20 per cent.

The addition of this brandy stops all fermentation. The unfermented sugar remains in the wine as sweetening. The wine is then drained off into large casks and stored. During this time, the wine is carefully watched and shipped down to Villa Nova Do Jaia, a small town across the bay from Oporto, where most of the shippers have their warehouses.

These shippers then blend ports of different characteristics to produce the types of wines for which the house is famous. Each one has its own system and formula of blending and some even add a little more brandy at this stage. The object of this blending is to maintain an established standard of quality.

After the original aging, should the wine develop into a big, fine wine capable of further improvement in the bottle, the wine will be bottled at once and sold as a vintage wine. If it does not meet these exacting requirements, it is usually stored away for a period varying between eight and twenty years.

The longer the port remains in wood, the more "tawney" it becomes. Port wine that has matured in the bottle has a deep, brilliant ruby color. Port wine that has matured in wood loses more and more color the longer it is kept and takes on a brownish, russet tinge. That is why it is called tawney. White ports are made in the same manner, only white grapes are used.

There are no château-bottled port wines, so that the tradition of the place of origin and the type of wine are less important than the name of the shipper and his reputation.

Port wine will be found to be excellent with fruit, cheese, cake, or after the dessert. An Englishman's favorite drink after lunch is a glass of fine port wine, while one of the most popular phrases heard in England is "A glass of port and a biscuit."

The different types of port wines are as follows.

Vintage Port

This Port is produced from wine of a single year and is made only during good vintage years. If it has the rigid requirements of a big, fine wine it will be aged in wood for two years and then bottled. The wine is usually allowed to develop in the bottle fifteen to twenty-five years before it becomes fully mature and ready for consumption. During its tenure in the bottle, the wine becomes more mellow and dry with a fine bouquet and aroma. Vintage ports are quite expensive, since the care and length of aging require much time on the part of the maker and a long period of investment. Vintage wines selling for very low prices should be looked upon with skepticism.

Crusted Port

This is a very fine wine matured in the bottle in the same manner as a vintage port, but the fermentation takes place partly in the barrel and partly in the bottle. Because of the fermentation in the bottle, a crust or sediment is formed from the settling out of the body of the wine. The crust is a common formation in this type of wine and great care must be taken when pouring in order that no part of the crust enter the glass. This crust or sediment is also characteristic of the vintage port wines. This crust is composed of argol, tartrate of lime, and other substances.

Tawney Port

Tawney port differs from the others in that it is kept in the wood for a long period and bottled only when it is ready to be shipped to market. The wine will be light in body and color and lower in alcoholic content, since the period spent in the cask has allowed the heavy body to settle out and some of the alcohol to evaporate. An authentic, rare, old tawney port will be quite expensive, since it is a blend of wines of the finest quality. Port by steady stages becomes, while in the cask, first ruby, then tawney, and finally light tawney, with the color and body becoming lighter in each stage.

Ruby Port

This a younger wine than the tawney, but is kept in the wood casks until bottling time for a much shorter period. The wine is a light red color, is sweeter than tawney, and not as smooth.

Geropiga Wine

This admirable wine, though produced in Spain and having much the same characteristics as port, cannot be marketed under that name. Geropiga is produced in the region around the town of Tarragone in southeastern Spain. This wine may be described as a kind of liqueur with a certain affinity to the Spanish Dulce and the French Rogommé, and is as well known as either. Geropiga is in much demand for giving character to low-class ports, besides being exported in considerable quantities to America. This wine, when of good quality, is composed of two-thirds or more of unfermented grape juice and one-third or more of over-proof grape brandy. In some varieties of Geropiga, the grape juice undergoes a partial fermentation which is checked by the addition of brandy. However made, it is commonly deepened in color with elderberry after which it is sweetened with grape sugar. This liqueur, for such it really is, costs about double the price of a good average port wine. The Geropiga comes in both the red and white varieties, each having a soft, fragrant, full-bodied character with a dry, fresh after-taste.

Hungarian Tokay

Tokay is the wine which has made Hungary famous, since the wine has been highly praised for its delightful fragrance and delicacy. Tokay is a sweet, light-bodied wine, yet in contrast to the other sweet wines of the world, it is not fortified by the addition of brandy.

In making Tokay, the perfectly dried berries, after being carefully selected, are placed in tubs the bottoms of which are pierced with holes to admit the juice exuding from the mere weight of the grapes resting upon each other, dripping into the vessel below. The liquid thus collected abounds in saccharine matter, and is known as the essenz. After the lapse of years, it is remarkable for its excessive lusciousness, the richness of its bouquet, and its powerful flavor.

It is commonly pretended that the essenz should remain many years in wood before it is bottled. Still, of those marketed, only a very small percentage attain the prescribed age and with it, the divine harmony of strength, richness and aroma which the Hungarians claim for this rare product of their soil.

The distinguishing characteristic of Tokay, apart from taste, is the considerable quantity of phosphoric acid it contains which no other wine except Malaga has in anything approaching the same proportion.

Tokayer Ausbruch is produced by pressing ripe grapes from which the shriveled berries have been already selected, and adding the must (juice) obtained from a certain quantity of dried grapes previously reduced to a pulp, either by being well trodden or by a machine. According to whether the wine is required to be sweet or dry, the quantity of dried grapes is added to or reduced. For a very sweet wine thirty gallons of must will be mixed with five tubs containing thirty gallons of dried berries, while for a wine less sweet, four or fewer tubs will be employed. Hence, it is that in the mystic language of the producers, Tokay Ausbruch will be described as wine of one, two, three, four, five tubs or in the Hungarian language, *puttynos*.

Szomorodner is made from grapes which have not had all the ripest berries selected from them, and which, after being subjected to pressure in sacks, are next crushed beneath the bare, brawny feet of stalwart Magyars, when the must which has been previously pressed is poured over them. This mixture is allowed to remain for several hours until it commences to ferment. After being stirred a few times, it is then placed in sacks and trodden. When the must obtained from it is poured into casks, the lees serve to make *vin ordinaire*. The quality of Szomorodner wine depends upon the amount of dry grapes used in the preparation. The general qualities of this wine are perfect softness and fullness, combined with that particular pungency common to every variety of Tokay. This wine is quite a bit drier than the essenz or Ausbruch varieties.

The Care of Wines

The ideal wine cellar should be underground, dark, dry, and with a constant temperature as near as possible to 55 degrees Fahrenheit. The cellar should be well ventilated and free from draughts and vibration. In country homes a corner of the cellar may be walled off and the above conditions maintained. The corner should be devoid of hotwater or heating pipes. Town apartments present greater difficulties. The solution advised is to select a closet, without heating pipes in the walls, and use it as a working cellar, keeping your principal stocks stored with your wine merchant.

Wine bins may be built like a honeycomb and fixed around the walls. Metal racks may be purchased for the purpose. In this manner the wine should not have to be disturbed until ready for use. All wines should be placed horizontally immediately on their receipt and remain unmoved until required. The wines are kept in this position so that the cork will be moist. Sparkling wines will go flat quickly if allowed to stand vertical. When a wine stands upright for a period, the cork will dry and then shrink. The shrinkage allows the air to enter the bottle and deteriorate the wine. Champagne and other white wines should be kept in the lower or cooler bins. The clarets and other red wines should occupy the next tier, while the ports, sherries, and Madeiras can be placed higher still. The latter need not be stored horizontally, since exposure to air does not harm a sweet fortified wine.

All wines, especially red wines, should remain tranquil for at least ten days before serving. The wines should be inspected regularly for leaking or ailing corks. These faulty bottles should be removed immediately since the damage often spreads. The leaking bottles must be recorked and if necessary filtered to remove bits of cork or sediment.

Many wine lovers usually find it interesting to keep a cellar book, noting entries, dates, costs and comments on the wine when used. This book will be a record of the wines used by the host and the comments entered will enable more advantageous purchasing in the future, since the wines most enjoyable will have the most favorable entries.

The Service of Wine

The voyage of a bottle of wine from the cellar to the wine glass, if conducted correctly, will take on the semblance of a ritual. The procedure may seem a little complicated, but the pleasure derived from serving a bottle of fine wine is enhanced by the care taken during the service.

The amount of care observed in serving a white or red wine will reduce the disturbance to the wine itself. Shaking or turning a wine, especially a red wine causes the sediment to cloud the wine and distort the color and brilliance. The use of a wine basket facilitates the voyage and reduces the amount of shaking and jarring that the bottle must undergo before it is served. If a wine basket is not used, slowly turn the bottle upright and keep it in that position until ready for service.

Decanting

Only wines containing sediment in quantity need be decanted. The bottle should remain in an upright position for at least twenty-four hours before decanting. While decanting a wine, use scrupulously clean instruments, pour evenly without halting, and stop at the first sign of sediment. It is unwise to decant more than one bottle at a time, since each bottle may have different characteristics. These may be lost when the two wines are decanted together.

Temperatures

The full flavor of a wine is more easily brought out if it is served at the correct temperature. Clarets and still red Burgundy should be served at room temperature. This is best accomplished by placing the wine in the dining room several hours before serving. Never warm a wine by artificial means, even if you are hurried. Leave the wine in the kitchen until it is required. White wines should be served chilled or iced depending on the sweetness of the wine. A great sweet white wine like Château d'Yquem should be thoroughly iced, while a great dry white wine like Montrachet Burgundy should only be chilled. Icing serves to conceal the failings of an inferior wine. Ice should never be put into any wine, only around the bottle. Champagne and other sparkling wines should be thoroughly iced, but not iced too long. If a wine is chilled too long, it will lose most of its flavor and bouquet. Usually chilling champagne in an ice bucket for about twenty minutes or on the bottom of a refrigerator for about an hour will bring the wine to the correct temperature.

Opening the Bottle

First, remove the foil from the neck of the bottle and also the wire and any other material that may come in contact with the wine during the pouring. Then wipe the lip of the bottle with a clean cloth. It is correct to wrap a napkin around the bottle to prevent any injury in case there is any flaw in the bottle which would cause it to break. Then insert the corkscrew and slowly withdraw the cork. Be careful not to disturb the wine or break the cork. The best type of corkscrew to use is one with a long, sturdy shank operated preferably by leverage. Then taste the wine to make sure it is worthy.

Glasses

The true lover of wine will avoid the use of fancy, colored, or eccentric shaped glasses. A proper wine glass is clear, thin, and very delicate, with a tulip shaped bowl of generous proportions, which is set on a graceful, slender stem. A modest but adequate glassware supply would include about six types and shapes of wine glasses. The wine glass should never be more than half full, permitting exposure of the wine to the air and the gathering of the bouquet. Connoisseurs often prefer a very large, paper-thin balloon glass to display a noble Burgundy or claret.

Enjoying Wine

Fine wines are enjoyed for their color, their fragrance, their taste, and the appreciation that follows drinking. Sip a fine wine, slowly, admiring its taste and other charms. Never drink a fine wine to quench the thirst. Use water for this purpose. It is not only proper but suggested that the host serve his own fine wines. The host should pour the first few drops into his own glass, so that any particles of cork in the wine will not be served to the guests.

Proper Wines To Serve With Food

As an Appetizer

Pale dry sherry, with or without bitters, chilled or not. Plain or mixed vermouth, with or without bitters. A dry cocktail.

With Oysters, Clams or Caviar

A dry flinty wine such as Chablis, Moselle, champagne.

With the Fish

Dry white Burgundy, Rhine, Moselle, or Alsace wines; dry champagne, or dry Graves.

With Entrees: Light Meats, Chicken, Lamb, Pork

Light red Burgundies, second to fifth-growth clarets, fine white Burgundies.

With Heavy Red Meats: Steak, Game, Duck, Beef

Full-bodied Burgundy, Côtes du Rhône, first growth claret, or champagne.

With the Dessert

Classified sauternes such as Château d'Yquem or Château Latour Blanche. Demi-sec champagne, full-bodied sweet port, sherry, or Madeira. Hungarian Tokay well chilled is excellent. Sparkling Burgundy or Sparkling Moselle.

With the Cheese

A glass of fine port wine served at room temperature.

With the After-Dinner Coffee

A fine cognac brandy or a glass of liqueur. After a heavy dinner a glass of Crème de Menthe will quickly put a person at ease.

With the Fruits and Nuts

Tawney, port wine, Tokay, Muscatel, or Madeira.

Customs Regarding Wine Service

There are several customs which should be observed when wines are served with food. They are not set rules, but if observed the enjoyment of good wines will be enhanced. These usages can be altered to meet your own taste if those suggested do not agree.

The host and his guests should always regard wines as an accompaniment to a certain type of food. Many people who have decided that they do not like a sweet wine such as Château d'Yquem, simply have neglected to serve this great wine with the right type of dessert. Château d'Yquem is best enjoyed when served with a not-too-sweet dessert. This linking with another type of food is true of all other wines. The host should not reserve the use of wines only to his formal dinners. The use of wine should be increased to a common occurrence. When wine is served there need not be five or six wines over the course of the dinner. If there is only one bottle of wine in the house, serve it. It will be correct and very enjoyable.

When serving several wines with a dinner, the effect to strive for is one of stepping through the lesser wines to the great wine, usually served with the game or roast. Red wines should never be served before white wines, nor a red Burgundy before a claret, or a sweet wine before a dry wine. Sweet wines should not be served through the course of the whole meal. Dry wines are reserved for this purpose, while the sweet wines should be served with the dessert or with fruit.

Vinegar and jelly are unfriendly when served with wines. Salads and dressings containing vinegar should be omitted from the dinner when wines are used. Red wines should be served with game, roasts, pork and other red meats. White wines are more enjoyable with fish, white meats, vegetables, oysters and shellfish.

A light white wine may be served throughout a simple meal and champagne may be served throughout any meal. Rhine, Moselle, champagne, and white Burgundies are ideal as summer luncheon wines.

Wines should not be drunk to quench the thirst. Sip them, admiring their taste, color and bouquet.

Brandy

The Types Of Brandy

Brandy is a distillation of fruit or grape wines. The finer products are usually blends of several different types of brandy, with each type donating its distinctive characteristics of body, aroma, flavor, quality, and age. Brandies are made from many different kinds of grapes and fruits, and each may have a great quality all its own, but still be entirely different from the other. When the word *brandy* is used unqualified by the additional name of a fruit, grape brandy is always understood.

The several types of brandy commonly known are:

Cognac Brandy

Brandy may be made from any wine produced in any part of the world. However, the finest grape brandy is cognac, which is distilled from wine made from grapes grown in that section of France known as the Charante district. The principal city is the ancient town of Cognac. The by-word for grape brandy all over the world is cognac. Only brandy made in the Charante district may be called cognac. Therefore all cognac is brandy, but not all brandy is cognac.

The large shippers of cognac brandies do not grow or distill all of the brandy they sell; on the contrary, the major part of the distilling is done by individual proprietors of vineyards who later sell the distilled product to the shippers. The grapes are picked in October, but distillation takes place usually in December.

The new brandy is placed in barrels of Limousin Oak. It is at that time a colorless liquid of very high proof. The oak imparts to the brandy a particular aroma and the beautiful golden hue which all cognac has. During the years that the cognac is maturing in the cask, it naturally loses strength and bulk by evaporation. The loss through aging is considerable, but there is no other way to age cognac or any other spirit. The air that the oak casks "breathe" through the cognac will in time change the raw spirit to a mellow, soft liqueur pleasing in color, bouquet, and taste.

All cognacs are blended. That is, brandies of varying ages and characteristics and produced in different sections of the Cognac region, are married together to produce a harmonious and balanced product.

49

Of the various districts of the Charante district, those producing the finest cognac in order of their quality are Grande Fine Champagne, the Petite Champagne, the Borderier, and the Premier Bois. The larger the percentage of Grande Fine Champagne and Petite Champagne in the blend, the finer the quality the brandy will be.

In America, the age statement of a cognac brandy has taken on far too much importance. Some of the finest brandies on the market have no age statement attached at all. Usually the unmarked cognac brandies have a designation which will denote the approximate quality.

Armagnac Brandy

Armagnac is a very fine brandy distilled from wine produced in the Department of Gers, just south of Bordeaux. A somewhat different practice is observed in the making of Armagnac; whereas, Armagnac is very often shipped as a vintage product (straight), cognac is always shipped blended.

Armagnac matures faster than cognac and up to twenty years of age may be superior to cognac. However, at an older age cognac is superior because it does not become quite so heavy in body. Armagnac is noted for its heavy body, smoothness, and bouquet.

Spanish Brandy

Spanish brandy is produced from fine sherry wine in the Jerez district of Spain. The brandy has the flavor and bouquet of sherry although it is not unlike cognac brandy. The brandy is highly regarded and in the older stocks is considered very excellent.

Apple Brandy

Apple brandy originated in the northwest section of France in the Province of Normandie, where the brandy is known as Calvados. The brandy is distilled from apple cider and aged in wooden barrels. In America the brandy is known as Applejack.

Slivovitz Brandy

Slivovitz is a brandy distilled from plums. It is usually produced in Hungary, Czechoslovakia, Yugoslavia, and Roumania. The brandy is aged in wood and has the distinct flavor of plums. Slivovitz is usually bottled at very high proof.

Kirsch or Kirschwasser

Kirsch is a brandy made from cherries grown in Switzerland, Alsace, France, Germany, and other sections. The brandy is very strong, being the direct distillation of the cherries, the pits included, with no syrups added. Kirsch is primarily used in cooking and mixed drinks.

Greek Brandy.

Greek brandy is outstanding because of the very heavy liquorous body and rich flavor. The brandy is very mellow and smooth to the taste.

Rum

Rum is one of the most versatile of all liquors. There are many types of rum and many more ways to use it. Rum is produced in most tropical parts of the world, with each distillation having its own characteristic body, aroma, and flavor.

Most rums are distilled from sugar cane which is first pressed and the juice fermented for several days. The fermented liquid is then distilled, rectified, and filtered, after which it is placed in enormous oak vats. The rum is permitted to mature in these vats at 150 proof.

The types of rum and their characteristics are:

Jamaica Rum

Jamaica rum is exceptionally popular, being used with tea, coffee, or as a base of cocktails. It has a fine distinctive quality, flavor, and heavy body all its own. Many Jamaica rums are shipped in large casks to the London docks on the banks of the Thames River where they are matured for at least three years. Jamaica rum is popular as a fine liqueur.

Cuban Rum

Cuban rum is milder, somewhat less fragrant, than Jamaica rum, and with a much lighter body. It is very famous as a base for innumerable cocktails. A rare Cuban rum has the characteristics of a fine brandy and may be used as a straight liqueur.

Martinique Rum

Martinique rum is made in the French West Indies and is quite similar to Jamaica rum, although not nearly so heavy in body and flavor.

Puerto Rico, Virgin Islands

These West Indies rums are light bodied and very similar to the Cuban rums.

New England Rum

New England Rum has been famous all over the world for hundreds of years. The manufacture of this rum dates back to the early days of the American colonies. This product, with usual variations has come down to the present date, still being produced in modest quantities for sale both here and abroad.

According to several sources, rum was first distilled in the Barbados Islands about 1640 to 1645. Its early name was "Kill-Devil." Later it was captioned "Rumbellion," a word which expressed the idea of a great quarrel or tumult. Then it was merely called Rum.

At the time rum was referred to as a hot, hellish and terrible liquor, but now with development for many years in wood, rum is very different, having become much smoother to the taste and fuller in body, aroma and flavor. This rum may be used for any purpose.

Demerara Rum

Demerara rum is produced in British Guiana. The essential differences between Demerara and Jamaica rums lie in the quality of the sugar cane and the different soil and climate of the two countries. Demerara rums are slightly darker and heavier in body. They do not possess the finesse or the bouquet of Jamaica, but there are those who prefer the more powerful Demerara rum. This rum is bottled at very high proof, sometimes as high as 150 proof (75%) alcohol by volume.

Arrack

Arrack is a type of rum which is distilled in Java, Siam, Jamaica, and East India. It is prepared by the distillation of fermented rice and molasses mash which is made from sugar cane. Another method of manufacture is distillation of the rice and the molasses mash along with Toddy, a palm wine obtained by the fermentation of the juice of the cocoanut palm.

The Arrack ranges in color from yellow to light brown. In flavor and aroma, it is very similar to the rums of the West Indies. The alcoholic content of Arrack ranges from 90 to 130 proof.

The main uses of this liquor are: in the preparation of hot drinks, the manufacture of Swedish Punch, and in the making of bitters.

Vodka

Genuine vodka is made from a mash of unmalted rye and either barley or rye malt. In the cheaper grades, however, potatoes or corn have been used. Vodka is the national drink of the Russians and the Poles. It is usually packed in bottles which are about three-quarters full and at an alcoholic content which ranges from 90 to 120 proof. In color and flavor vodka resembles the dry type of gin.

Liqueurs

Centuries ago, liqueurs were originated by alchemists, from whom we have obtained many of the fine liqueurs we now enjoy.

Liqueurs, as a class, are of foreign origin and manufacture and their terminology is somewhat confusing. In this country the names "liqueur" and "cordial" are practically interchangeable. Abroad liqueurs generally are products made on the continent and especially in France, while cordials are products originating in the United Kingdom and elsewhere. Another possible distinction is that the liqueurs as a group are more perfume-like in character and exclude the cordials which are made with much sharper flavors.

In making of liqueurs there is a very wide field wherein to exercise ingenuity to give the product practically any shade or color to attract the attention and raise curiosity. There can be used countless fruits, seeds, nuts, herbs and spices with which to please even the most fastidious taste.

There are two main methods by which liqueurs may be made, namely, the infusion method and the maceration method. Almost all of the fruit liqueurs such as peach, apricot, cherry, etc., are made by the infusion method. According to the infusion method a certain proportion of the fresh fruit is steeped in a barrel or vat of fine brandy for about one year. The brandy will have then absorbed all of the flavor, bouquet and color of the fruit that was infused in it. When the spirit is drawn off, it is then filtered and sweetened with syrup. The liqueur is then ready for bottling.

The plant liqueurs are made by the maceration method. The ingredients of the liqueur are steeped in fine brandy for two days. Then the contents of the whole vat are distilled. The resulting distillation has all the properties of taste and bouquet of the spices, herbs and seeds first used. Since all distillations are colorless, most of the plant liqueurs are brilliantly colored, artificially. Examples of these liqueurs are Crème de menthe, Crème de Cocoa and Crème de Roses.

Liqueurs are mainly used as after-dinner drinks, since they are sweet and potent. However, during recent years, there were invented numberless cocktails and mixtures calling for various liqueurs as ingredients. Notable among these cocktails are the Sidecar, calling for Triple Sec; Alexander, calling for Crème de Cocoa, and the Stinger, calling for Crème de Menthe.

The following is a list of the different types of liqueurs and their main ingredients.

Anisette

A crystal clear, white liqueur distilled from anise seed, bitter almonds, coriander and several other ingredients. Anisette may be used as an after-dinner liqueur or as a base or flavoring agent for numerous cocktails.

Absinthe

This popular French drink is now prohibited all over the world because of its evil effects, mainly because of the presence of the drug wormwood in the Absinthe. Several fine substitutes are marketed under different names since no product may bear this name. Those products are safe and definitely not harmful since none of them contain wormwood. These products are known as Pernod's "Liqueur Veritas" or "Anise," "Herbsainte," produced in New Orleans by Legendre, Spanish "Ojen" and several others. The main ingredients are hyssop, lemon balm, green Anise, Chinese aniseed, fennel, coriander, and several other roots and herbs.

Apricot, Cherry, Blackberry and Peach

These liqueurs are made by steeping the fresh fruit in fine brandy for about a year, then straining off the liqueur and sweetening with sugar syrup.

Benedictine

Produced by the Benedictine Monks at Fécamp, France, from a secret formula since 1510, the liqueur was dedicated to God with the Latin words deo optimo maximo which means, 'To God, most good, most great.' Benedictine is made from a large number of plants, seeds and herbs, some of which grow in the vicinity of Fécamp and many that come from far-off countries, together with the finest brandy. Among the many ingredients used, the most common are: cloves, nutmeg, cinnamon, peppermint, angelica root, alpine mugwort, aromatic calamus, cardamon, and flowers of arnica.

Crème de Ananas

This fine, smooth liqueur is made by infusing fresh pineapple in brandy and later flavoring with vanilla.

Crème de Cocoa

Crème de Cocoa is made from cocoa beans, cloves, mace and vanilla. This liqueur has a distinct chocolate flavor and is the main ingredient of the Alexander cocktail.

Crème de Cassis

This popular French Liqueur is made from black currants, spirit of strawberries and an infusion of wild cherries. This liqueur is used in making the very popular French drink, Vermouth Cassis.

Crème de Banana

A smooth, sweet liqueur made from an infusion of fresh Martinique bananas and brandy.

Crème de Moka

This liqueur is made from coffee beans and brandy and is marketed in either a white or brown color.

Crème de Noyaux

A rare liqueur made by steeping a combination of apricot stones, cherry stones, dried peach leaves, myrrh and nutmeg along with brandy. This liqueur has the flavor of almonds.

Crème de Roses

An exotic liqueur produced from essence of roses or rose water made from roses grown on the hills of Nice. The rose petals lend a delightful fragrance and color to the liqueur.

Crème de Violette

The *Violettes* grown near Monte Carlo are the main ingredients of this liqueur.

Crème de Vanilla

This liqueur is made by infusing vanilla beans in brandy. Its main uses are in cooking and in the preparation of cocktails.

Channelle

A rare liqueur made from cinnamon and several other spices.

Chartreuse

The Grand Chartreuse is now made at Tarragona, Spain, by the Chartreux Monks. The formula has been a secret for centuries, but the yellow chartreuse is reputed to have 18 different ingredients and the green chartreuse about 250. The liqueur has been imitated many times, but the only authentic Chartreuse is made at Tarragona, Spain, and Paris, France. Some of the main plants, roots, herbs and flowers used are: Melisse citronne, hyssop flowers, dry peppermint, alpine mugwort, balsamite, thyme, angelica leaves, arnica flowers, mace, Chinese aniseed, coriander aloes, cloves, cardamom, and many others.

Cointreau

Cointreau is a brand of Triple Sec orange curacao and world famous as a liqueur and the base of the Sidecar cocktail.

Cordial Médoc

The ingredients of this fine liqueur are curacao orange, fine champagne, cognac and claret from the Médoc district of France.

Crème de Fine Champagne

A rare liqueur made from several fine cordials blended with fine champagne cognac.

Crème de Menthe

A peppermint liqueur made from fresh mint leaves macerated in brandy spirits. This fine liqueur is marketed in three different colors: green, red and white. In France, crème de menthe is usually consumed as a highball. In recent years this liqueur has become famous as one of the ingredients of the Stinger cocktail.

Crème de Recco

A very fine liqueur, quite unknown, made by macerating tea leaves in brandy and sweetening with sugar syrup.

Crème de Célérie

Made from either spirit or essence of celery infused with brandy. One of the rarest liqueurs made.

Liqueur de Dessert

Dessert liqueur is usually made in Italy and called either Strega or Galliano. The ingredients of this very fine plant liqueur are: Angelica seed, calamus, Ceylon cinnamon, myrrh, cloves, aloes, vanilla, nutmeg, saffron, sugar and brandy.

Drambuie

This is the most famous of the English liqueurs. Drambuie has a base of very fine old Scotch whisky. The other ingredients are honey and many other herbs and spices. Drambuie has been produced since 1745 and is called "Prince Charles Edwards Scotch Liqueur."

Curacao

One of the most popular liqueurs in the United States is orange curacao which is marketed in the familiar tall stone jug. This liqueur is made chiefly from the peel of the bitter curacao orange. These oranges grow chiefly in the West Indies and the price for genuine curacao peels is quite high, so that the distillers usually substitute up to 50 per cent of other cheaper bitter orange peels in the cheaper liqueurs sold.

The main ingredients of the genuine curacao are: fresh curacao orange peels, fresh orange peels of another type of orange, cloves, mace, Jamaica rum, port wine, sugar syrup and brandy or spirits.

Fraise

A liqueur made from strawberries steeped in fine brandy.

Framboise

A liqueur made from raspberries steeped in fine brandy.

Flora Alpina

This Italian liqueur is also called Flora Di Alpe and Flora Delle Alpe. It is made from various herbs and spices, most prominent of which is the Alpine flower or Edelweiss plant. This liqueur is marketed in a tall, tapering bottle with a small tree covered with crystalized rock-candy inside. Three different types are made, namely: red, orange and yellow.

Grand Marnier

Grand Marnier is a blend of fine champagne cognac and orange curacao, and is world famous as an after-dinner liqueur, as a flavoring agent in cooking, and as the base for many fine cocktails.

Forbidden Fruit

This is the only American liqueur which is exported to Europe. It is made from the fruit of the shaddock tree, which bears a type of grape-fruit. The shaddock is steeped in fine imported French cognac and marketed in a distinctive gold crowned bottle.

Elixir de Bacardi

A Cuban liqueur made principally from rum.

Goldwasser

This liquer is also known as Eau de Vie de Danzig and Golden Elixir. In France, it is called *liqueur d'or,* or 'liqueur of gold.' This fascinating liqueur contains tiny flakes of gold leaf which, when agitated, give the liqueur an exotic appearance. The main ingredients of Goldwasser are: Ceylon cinnamon, ripe figs, cumin, musk seed, mace, cloves and lemon peel macerated in brandy and then distilled.

Kaymagui or Kaluah

A Mexican coffee liqueur made from coffee beans and cocoa beans macerated in fine brandy, then distilled and sweetened with sugar syrup and flavored with vanilla. It is many times served as an after-dinner liqueur or as a demi-tasse, that is, half and half with sweet cream.

Kirschwasser

Cherry brandy made from the pits of cherries distilled with brandy and flavored with orange flower water.

Kummel

A liqueur made from caraway seeds and brandy. The dry type should be served well chilled.

Maraschino Liqueur

A very popular liqueur made from Marasca cherries grown on the west coast of the Adriatic Sea in a district called Dalmatia. Maraschino may be used as a liqueur, as flavoring in cooking and in many different cocktails.

Mandarine

Liqueur made by macerating the small mandarine orange in brandy.

Mirabelle

Made from the mirabelle, a type of yellow plum grown in Alsace, France.

Pousse Café

A blend of many different cordials.

Prunelle

A liqueur made from prunes or sloes, a type of plum.

Parfait Amour

Meaning 'perfect love,' an exotic liqueur having a beautiful royal purple color. The main ingredients are essence of lemon, oranges, coriander, anise and brandy and sugar syrup.

Cent Sept Ans

'107 years' — A very rare liqueur produced in France. The main ingredients are: spirit of lemon, rose water, orchil and brandy.

Punch Liqueur

Very rare liqueur made in France or Holland. The main ingredients are: brandy, tafia, spirit of lemon, citric acid, hyswen tea, burnt sugar and water.

Quince Brandy

Also called Ratafia de Coings. The main ingredients of this very rare liqueur are: sweet juice of ripe quinces, spirit of cloves and brandy.

Trapistine

A very rare liqueur of the plant family, the main ingredients of which are: grand pernod's, angelica, peppermint, cardamon, melisse, myrrh, calamus, cinnamon, cloves, mace and brandy.

Vespetro

A plant liqueur whose main ingredients are: amber seeds, dill, anis, caraway, coriander, daucas, fennel and brandy.

Sloe Gin

Sloe gin is not a gin, but a lovely, mild, after-dinner liqueur. It is made from the sloe berry.

Vieille Cure

Vieille Cure is a plant liqueur made in France whose ingredients are secret.

Advocaat

Fresh egg yolks preserved in fine brandy and sweetened with sugar. This excellent and nutritious liqueur has been produced in Holland for many hundreds of years.

Whiskies

Scotch Whiskies

The whiskies produced in Scotland are made primarily from malted barley. In contrast, United States and Canadian whiskies are made from corn, rye and wheat. Scotch whiskies are aged in casks which have contained sherry, whereas American whiskies are aged in charred oak casks.

The processes entered into during the production of Scotch whisky are divided into malting, mashing, fermenting, distilling, maturing, and blending.

Malting

In starting the malting process, the barley is first pressed and when required for use it is steeped in water and spread out on the malting floor for about three weeks. During this time the barley is sprinkled with water, the moisture causing the barley to sprout. When the sprouts are about three-quarters of an inch long, the water is turned off and the grain becomes known as malt. The malt is then dried over a peat fire with pungent smoke impregnating the malt with the peat flavor and aroma that is even evident after fermentation and distillation.

Mashing

The peat-dried malt is ground, after which it is transferred to the mash vat and soaked in hot water. After soaking, the ground malt is removed, the liqueur having absorbed all the goodness and flavor.

Fermentation

The liquid known as the "wort" is run into fermenting vats, after which a small quantity of very fine yeast is added and the fermentation takes place. The result is known as "beer."

Distillation

The beer is distilled and the resultant distillate is redistilled. The choice part of this second distillation is Scotch whisky.

Maturing and Blending

The new whisky is placed in sherry casks and then left to mature for about three years. After this period it is old enough to be blended or married with other Scotch whiskies. After blending, the whisky is again placed in the sherry casks for another four or five years or more before bottling.

Practically all Scotch whisky is blended, since most malt whiskies are too heavy to be palatable without tempering with neutral spirits. The finer the whisky, the smaller the quantity of grain whisky in the product. This is also true of the quantity of Highland malt whiskies in comparison to Lowland and Campbelltown malt whiskies in the blend. However, there are on the market, though few in number, some straight unblended malt whiskies. Most of the straight Scotches are produced at the famous Glenlivet Distillery. The straight malt whiskies have a very distnictive smoky flavor and heavy smooth body.

Irish Whiskey

Irish whiskey is a fine smooth liquor produced in the same manner as Scotch whisky, but does not have the smoky flavor. It is said that the connoisseur will not miss the smoky flavor in the least, since a good Irish whiskey over six years old is one of the finest and most satisfying liquors made. People drinking Irish whiskey doubt the alcoholic content although it is really 86 proof.

American Whiskey

The production of whiskies in the United States has been centered in five or six states, with the most famous being Kentucky, for its bourbon, and Maryland and Pennsylvania, for their rye whiskies. The people of this country, after going through prohibition, have developed, for the greater part, into drinkers of whiskies and other spirit liquors. Of all these distilled liquors, bourbon and rye predominate in the demand.

The whiskies produced in this country are classified as "rye," "bourbon," or "corn" whiskies. Bourbon is made from a mixture of corn, rye, wheat, oats, and barley, with corn making up at least 51 per cent of the total. Rye whiskey is made from rye and other grains, with rye making up at least 51 per cent of the total. Corn whiskey is made from corn with just enough barley malt added to aid in conversion. Barley malt is used in all of the above whiskies to aid in the conversion during fermentation.

The production of whiskey is made up of six different operations: preliminary treatment of raw materials, mashing, yeasting, fermentation, distillation, and maturing.

Materials

The materials from which whiskey is produced are grains such as: rye, corn, oats, barley malt, and wheat. Rye and corn predominate in the preparation of the grain mash. On account of the firm structure of the kernels, the raw grain must first be ground into meal and then cooked to make it readily soluble to the enzymes during mashing.

Mashing

In the making of corn or rye whiskey a certain series of processes is required by which the starchy raw materials are prepared for yeast production or fermentation. For every bushel of grain twenty to twenty-five gallons of water are added to the mash. The mash is then thoroughly stirred and allowed to stand overnight, during which time a small amount of lactic acid forms to give the mash a sour or acid characteristic. The mash is then brought to the boiling point, and maintained for about fifteen minutes. The mash is allowed to cool to about 150 degrees and the barley malt added for the purpose of liquefying the starch. The temperature is thereby reduced to 140 degrees called the malting or conversion point. It is held at this temperature from fifteen minutes to an hour, during which time the greater portion of the starch is converted to sugar. The mash is then ready for fermenting.

Yeasting

Yeast is a single-cell vegetable organism which reproduces itself under favorable conditions by budding. The four important essentials needed for the development and reproduction of yeast cells are: a supply of fermentable material, a supply of yeast food in the form of minerals, an ample supply of oxygen, and proper temperature conditions. Pure yeast is first cultured under favorable conditions at the distillers' laboratory. Yeasting is the process of adding the yeast to the prepared mash to induce fermentation.

Fermentation

During the mashing process, the starch has been converted into sugar which is readily fermentable. The fermentation process decomposes the sugar by means of certain enzymes, resulting in the transformation of the sugars into alcohol and carbonic acid gases. Under the sweet mash method of fermentation the period of fermentation is limited by federal statute to seventy-two hours and not more than forty-five gallons of beer to each bushel of grain. The sour mash process in which the time of fermentation must not exceed ninety-six and not more than sixty gallons of beer per bushel of grain, produces a whiskey heavier in body and richer in flavor than the sweet mash method. In the early stages of the fermentation, there is a rapid development of the yeast. Carbonic acid gas bubbles break the surface of the mass, forming a thickening cap of foam. The whole mass then comes into vigorous motion. The temperature rises and the main fermentation takes place, the sugar being transferred into alcohol.

Distillation

The fermented mash then enters into the distilling process for the purpose of separating the high volatile liquid from the low volatile liquid and a nonvolatile substance. The fermented mash is put through the still where the alcohol is separated from the slop and beer.

Bottled in Bond Whisky

Whiskies bottled in bond under the supervision of the United States government must conform to the strictest regulations on the bottling and labeling in the world. The whiskey must be at least four years old, of one distillation, bottled at 100 proof, and distilled, aged, and bottled under government supervision. No spirit whiskey may be added to defray shrinkage, nor can coloring material be added. Government regulations also specify that all whiskies again in bonded warehouses must be tax paid, and removed after eight years of aging.

Maturing

The aging of whiskey depends upon time and temperature. Newly distilled whiskey is practically colorless and has a crude, unpleasant flavor. By storing it in charred oak barrels certain changes occur which transform the whiskey into an amber, mellow liquid higher in proof.

Prolonged storage results in a loss in bulk and an increase in the alcoholic content. Loss in volume is a result of evaporation through the pores of the oak cask in an action called "breathing." There is no noticeable loss in the esters, aldehydes, furfural, acids, or fusel oil during the storage, but there is an increase in acids and esters which reach equilibrium after the fourth year.

Rye whiskies were, as a rule, aged in heated warehouses where the changes taking place were aided by the higher temperature. This higher temperature increased the loss in volume. Bourbon whiskies on the other hand were, as a rule, aged in unheated warehouses so that there was less loss in volume, less increase in proof, and less chemical change.

Whiskey aged in uncharred casks lacks the aromatic flavor peculiar to American whiskey, resembling more the flavor of Scotch, but lacking the smoky flavor.

Bourbon Whiskey

The first whiskey distilled in Kentucky was produced from corn, which was grown on the small farms where these stills were set up. Later it was found that the introduction of some rye with the corn in the mash increased the yield of spirits produced, and improved the flavor. Still later it was found that barley, malted, further increased the yield.

The fertile county of Bourbon was by far the largest producer of Whiskey in Kentucky in the early days, and it is said that the first still was erected there. The whiskey made in that county became known as "bourbon" whiskey. Later other counties became celebrated for the quantity and quality of their whiskey, such as: Nelson, Anderson, Fayette, Daviess and Marion. During the Civil War the county in which the whiskey was made became the trademark for all the distilleries in that county. Later the County of Bourbon, being the largest producer of whiskey, became the most important source of supply for the demand for the goods from outside the state. Consequently Kentucky whiskey was linked with the name of the county from which it came. Later bourbon became the generic term for all whiskies made in the State of Kentucky of which the largest percentage of grain from which it was made consisted of corn.

After having successfully established a legitimate commerce with bourbon whiskey, the distillers began to manufacture other whiskey with a large percentage of rye grain and sometimes with a total of rye, known as rye whiskey, so that for more than thirty years all whiskey made in Kentucky has been known as either bourbon or rye whiskey.

Sour Mash Kentucky Bourbon Whiskey

In the old methods of making sour mash whiskey, the cream of the grains used was sought, and not a method of deriving a larger quantity of spirit out of a bushel. This whiskey is regarded as the finest produced and is usually produced under the old hand-made sour mash method.

Pure mountain spring water at 56 degrees Fahrenheit is used for mash, blending and general use in a distillery of this type. If insufficient quantity is produced in the surrounding counties, the grains come from Minnesota (barley), Wisconsin (rye), and corn from various other midwestern states. The grain is cut between two stones by the old-fashioned way. The ground meal is put into an open barrel tub and thoroughly scalded with hot water. The stirring is done by hand with a rake and the barrel is then set aside to rest for twenty-four hours. At this time the grain is the consistency of mush.

The mush is raked again and thrown into the large fermenters. This is thinned down with hot water or strained slop so that the content of the fermenters is about one barrel of water to about one bushel of grain. The required proportion of small grain is added during the breaking up of the mush and the fermentation is started by skimming off sufficient quantity from the top of the fermenters during the seventy to ninety-six hours they are permitted to ferment. After the period of fermentation the fermenters become quiet. The starch in the corn has turned to beer, and is just as sour and tastes very much like it.

The beer is then pumped into a wooden three-chambered still and distilled into whiskey. This process separates the alcohol from the mash, leaving the slop behind. The Whiskey then finds its way to a second fermentation in a copper still heated over a wood fire. The distillation is so controlled that it boils over and runs into a cistern room at the bonded warehouse into a tank at 100 to 102 proof, so that the distiller can fill it into barrels at this proof without reducing with water. A good test of quality is that this whiskey, as it runs into the cistern room, is sweet, pleasant to the tase and smell.

The whiskey during aging is expected to increase in proof over that at which it was barreled. Most distillers of sour mash bourbons heat their warehouses in cold weather. To hold temperatures of warehouses too high is also disadvantageous, as it deprives whiskey of its natural development, impregnates it with too much tannic acid and deprives it of part of its bouquet.

Sour mash whiskies, are full of essential oils. Ninety-six hours of fermenation, and primitive methods all add to make the sour

mash whiskies heavier than other whiskies. They take, in conse-
quence, longer to mature and are hardly fit to drink before four years
old. From that time on they become mellowed in taste and finer in
flavor.

Rye Whiskey

Choice, mild, mellow and matured rye whiskey is the finest drink
man is capable of distilling from grain. Bismark once said, "Beer
is for women, wine for men, and rye for heroes."

Perpendicular drinking leads to oblique vision. It is recom-
mended that rye whiskey should never be consumed hurriedly. To
drink rye hurriedly is a sacrilege. Rye whiskey should be drunk slowly,
admiring the bouquet and fragile yet robust flavor. This whiskey is
one of the sweetest whiskies it is possible to distill.

At the present time rye whiskey must be composed with at least
50 per cent rye grain, with corn and other small grains making up
the balance. Individual distilleries, however, have their own formulas
and the percentage of rye grain to the others often runs up to 90 per
cent rye grain. Rye whiskey finds its greatest use in the mixing of
cocktails and highballs since this lighter, sweeter whiskey makes a
finer tasting drink than bourbon whiskey.

Gin, Beer and Bitters

The Types Of Gin

London Dry Gin

This gin is dry, bland, and moderately aromatic. It is made from distilled grain and redistilled with juniper, angelica, and other spices and herbs, depending upon the maker's formula. All spirits, no matter how pure, will differ slightly, due to the mineral content of the water used in the mash. Even though the identical procedure is used in the distillation, a spirit distilled in London will still differ in taste from a spirit distilled in America. An English-made gin has been proven on many occasions to have more finesse, a more delicate flavor, and mellower taste.

Old Tom Gin

Old Tom Gin is highly aromatic and made in the same manner as London dry gin, but with sweetening added. It is usually darker in color than dry gin. Sugar is less necessary in drinks made with Old Tom Gin.

Plymouth Gin

Plymouth gin in a combination of dry and Old Tom Gin being slightly sweet, but not as sweet as Old Tom Gin.

Holland Gin

Holland gin is a rich, aromatic highly flavored spirit. The mash is made from grain with a certain amount of rye grain and other spices added during distillation. Holland gin has its own distinctive flavor and is seldom used in cocktails.

German Gin

German gin is produced from grain mash with a certain percentage of rye grain along with other spices and herbs.

Fruit Flavored Gin

Fruit flavored gin is made from a regular gin base with the fruit flavor added during the distillation process. This gin is made in various fruit flavors.

Sloe Gin

Sloe gin is not a gin but a liqueur. It is made from sloe berries, has a red-brown color, and is quite sweet.

Syrups And Bitters

Grenadine

Grenadine is a syrup made from fresh pomegranates. It is usually nonalcoholic and mainly used in cocktails to give them color and to take the place of sugar. Grenadine is a light red color.

Gomme Syrup

Gomme Syrup is a simple syrup or simply sugar syrup. It is used in the making of drinks in place of sugar.

Orgeat Syrup

Orgeat syrup is a combination of simple syrup and bitter almonds. Recipes for many cocktails call for this syrup.

Framboise

Framboise is a raspberry syrup; fraise is a strawberry syrup, both being used as flavoring in cooking and in the making of cocktails. Blackberry syrup is also in this class.

Falernum

Falernum is a flavoring used in the preparation of rum cocktails.

Orange Bitters

Orange bitters is made from dried orange peels mixed with various flavoring and other aromatic agents. It is used extensively as a flavoring in making cocktails.

Fernet Bitters

Fernet is a type of stomach bitters made in Italy from various herbs and plants.

Boonekamp Bitters

Boonekamp is a type of stomach bitters made in Germany.

Angostura Bitters

Angostura bitters are used in cooking, in the making of cocktails and as a stomach bitter.

Orange Flower Water

Orange flower water is excellent as a flavoring in the preparation of cocktails.

Beer

The chief base of most beer is barley malt. American beers are made with an admixture of other grains, since American barley has a higher albumen content that German barley. For this purpose rice and corn are used after being freed from the husks.

American Beer

In the production of beer, the barley is malted first: that is, the grain, under moist heat, is allowed to sprout to a certain degree. Then the malt is ground, mixed with water and stirred under certain conditions and adjustments of temperature to extract and modify the solid constituents of the grain. The mash, as it is now called, has added to it the corn and rice, after being boiled separately.

The liquid called *wort* is then run off from the tub into a copper kettle and boiled for a certain period. While it is boiling the hops are added. The hops give aroma and taste and act as a natural preservative. The wort is then run over coolers into fermenting tanks and admixed with yeast. The yeast is the ferment which splits up the sugar into carbonic acid and alcohol, just as it does in bread, only in wort it acts more strongly. When the desired fermentation is reached, the wort is run into casks to undergo secondary fermentation and to allow the solids to settle out.

When the beer has reached the degree of aging and clarification that is necessary, it is racked or filled off into shipping packages. during the storing period most of the carbonic gas has escaped, and in order to restore the life and sparkle which depends upon the gas, some young wort is added before the beer is filled into the package. That is, the beer is carbonated and is also filtered before going into the packages.

English Beer

Credit for the invention of brewing is given to King Osiris of Egypt. Many records of this fact have been found in the great pyramids of that country.

The greatest brewing center in England is situated at Burton-on-Trent, where many famous brands of ale and stout are made. The trend is away from the heavy, potent stouts to the delicate pale ales.

Burton-on-Trent lies in a basin of marl and gypsum, which strongly impregnate the water collected in the brewery wells. The water is therefore very hard and of great benefit in the production of ale, since the water will not extract too much from the ale and not dissolve too much organic substance which is unwanted in the ale.

Soft water, unsuitable for ale, is suitable for the production of stout because it extracts more from the malt than hard water. Stout is usually made in Dublin where the water is of the soft type.

The best grain suited to the brewing of beer is barley and much depends upon the quality of the soil that grows it as well as on the wetness or dryness of the season. All barley will not make good malt and the choicest growths of barley at home and abroad are desired by the distillers of ale and stout.

The operations used in the making of the ale begin with malting. The barley is placed in shallow cisterns where it is steeped in water and afterwards spread out to the depth of a few inches on drying floors.

The barley is warmed gently and under the influence of warmth and moisture soon begin to sprout. After a certain specified time, the barley is dried by the kiln. If it is dried at low temperature, the malt will be termed pale malt, from which pale ale is brewed, but, if roasted at a greater heat, it is partially carbonized and becomes brown malt, suitable for brewing stout. This is the only reason for the difference in color between ale and stout.

The malt is then crushed between heavy rollers to break the husk and then is mixed with warm water. After mixing well, the mixture is termed *wort*. The wort is strained off from the insoluble portion of the malt and transferred to copper vats where it is boiled for several hours with the hops.

After sufficient boiling the wort is rapidly cooled in a refrigerator. The cooled wort, still unlike beer, is treated with yeast in order to induce fermentation and produce alcohol from the saccharine content of the beer. The yeast transforms the dull, lifeless wort into sparkling, zestful ale. The newly born ale is racked into casks and stored away in vast quantities for aging. English beers are equally bright and refreshing to the palate as Vienna or Bavarian beers, but do not froth so much.

Austrian Beer

Austrian beer, like all light beers of Germany, are brewed in accordance with the Bavarian system, and are generally a very superior beverage. They are of a pale amber color, exceedingly bright and sparkling and of a full, pleasant flavor, entirely free of acidity, and remarkably light drinking. The marked difference between Austrian, English and German beers lies principally in the brewing. Austrian beer is not nearly so strong as English beer, but yet it is fuller and more refreshing. Owing to its lightness, four times the quantity can be consumed as could be partaken of English beer without the risk of getting intoxicated or drowsy.

These beers have a very small amount of alcohol and are free from aldehydes and fusil oil. The beer usually runs 7 to 9 per cent and does not remain perfect for any length of time after being removed from the ice cellars because of the low percentage of spirit.

German beer of the Bavarian Province leads among the beer-producing states of Germany both in respect to the quantity and the quality of the beer brewed there. Bavarian beers are generally of a brilliant color and of a pleasant refreshing flavor.

Mixed Drinks

Correct Bar Procedure

1. Use good ingredients at all times.
2. Use correct glassware as noted in recipe.
3. Glassware should be clean and dry.
4. Cocktail glasses should be chilled with shaved ice before serving.
5. Shake drinks vigorously and serve very cold.
6. Do not use the ice a second time.
7. Super fine sugar will make clearer drinks.
8. Follow recipes carefully.
9. Mixed drinks should not stand too long before serving.
10. In order to frost a glass, first chill it with ice, then wet the inside rim with a small piece of lemon, and dip the glass into powdered sugar.
11. Measuring devices to be used are as follows:
    (a) Jigger—1½ ounces.
    (b) Pony—¾ ounce.
    (c) Bar Spoon—equal to ½ teaspoon.
    (d) Dash—equal to 20 drops or ¼ teaspoon.
    (e) Gill—equal to 4 ounces.
12. Sugar syrup may be used in the same proportions as dry sugar. A spoon of a dry ingredient should be level, not heaping.
13. Lemons may be substituted for limes, but avoid the use of the peel of the lime in a drink, since it has an unpleasant taste.
14. Cut peel for garnish as thinly as possible and never place in the drnik. Hang it over the eldge of the glass.
15. When stirring a drink, use a bar glass one-half full of shaved ice.
16. If stronger drinks are desired, stir them. Shaking makes drinks weaker.
17. The three forms of ice to be used in mixing are:
    (a) Shaved Ice—cut from cakes of ice with shaver.
    (b) Cracked Ice—placed in towel and cracked with hammer.
    (c) Cubed Ice—made in electric refrigerator.
18. Never add more bitters, liqueurs or syrups than are called for. A drink may be easily spoiled by too little or too much bitters.

Cocktails

Absent Cocktail

(Small Bar Glass)
Fill Bar Glass wth cracked ice
3 to 4 dashes Gomme Syrup
1 dash Angostura Bitters
2 dashes Orange Curacao
¼ pony water
¾ pony Pernod's
Shake well
Twist Lemon Peel on top

Absent No. 2

(Small Bar Glass)
¾ glass shaved ice
4 to 5 dashes Gomme Syrup
1 pony Pernod's
1 jigger water
Shake well
Strain into a Champagne Glass

Absent and Egg

⅓ jigger Pernod's
½ White of one Egg
⅓ Gin
1 scant spoon Sugar
Shake with ice till frosted
Serve in Cocktail Glass

Absent Frappe

(6 oz. Glass)
1 teaspoon Benedictine
1 jigger Pernod's
Shake well with ice — strain
Fill with plain soda

Absent French

(Cocktail Glass)
Fill glass with shaved ice
Place ½ lump Sugar on top
Drip 1 jigger Pernod's on sugar
Twist Lemon Peel on top
Serve with cut straws

Absent Frozen

(Highball Glass)
1 pony Pernod's
1 teaspoon Sugar Syrup
Shake well with ice
Strain into glass — add cracked ice
Fill with Seltzer

Absent Italian

1 pony Pernod's
½ pony Anisette
3 dashes Maraschino
½ pony water
Shake with ice until frosted
Strain into Cocktail Glass

Absent Martini

⅔ Dry Gin
⅓ French Vermouth
1 tablespoon Pernod's
Strain and serve in Cocktail Glass

Absent New Orleans

(Highball Glass)
1 jigger Whiskey
1 dash Angostura Bitters
1 dash Orange Bitters
1 dash Anisette
½ lump Sugar
2 dashes Pernod's
Shake well — strain
Twist Lemon Peel on top

Absent and Water

(Large Bar Glass)
1 pony Pernod's
Allow cold water to slowly drip into
    glass until full

Adelle Special

½ pony Orange Curacao
½ pony Scotch
Serve in Pony Glass

Admiral Cocktail

¾ jigger Dry Gin
1 spoon Cherry Cordial
½ spoon Lime Juice
½ spoon Sugar
Shake well
Strain into Cocktail Glass

Adonis Cocktail

1 dash Orange Bitters
⅓ Italian Vermouth
⅔ Dry Sherry
Stir well
Strain into Cocktail Glass

Affinity Cocktail—No. 1

⅓ French Vermouth
⅓ Italian Vermouth
⅓ Scotch Whisky
2 dashes Angostura Bitters
Shake well
Strain into Cocktail Glass
Twist Lemon Peel on top

Affinity Cocktail—No. 2

⅖ jigger Italian Vermouth
⅖ jigger French Vermouth
⅕ jigger Crème de Violette
Shake well
Strain into Cocktail Glass

After-Dinner Cocktail

½ Prunelle Liqueur
½ Cherry Liqueur
4 dashes Lemon Juice
Shake well
Strain into Sherry Glass

After-Dinner Special

½ Apricot Liqueur
½ Orange Curacao
Shake well
Serve in Cocktail Glass

After-Supper Cocktail

½ Apricot Liqueur
½ Orange Curacao
4 dashes Lemon Juice
Shake well
Strain into Sherry Glass

Alaska Cocktail

¾ Dry Gin
¼ Yellow Chartreuse
Shake well
Strain into Cocktail Glass

Albertine Cocktail

(Serves 6 people)
2 jiggers Kirschwasser
2 jiggers Cointreau
2 jiggers Chartreuse
2 dashes Maraschino
Shake well
Strain into Cocktail Glass

Alexander's Sister

⅓ Dry Gin
⅓ Crème de Menthe
⅓ Sweet Cream
Shake well
Strain into Cocktail Glass

Alexander Cocktail—No. 1

½ Dry Gin
¼ Crème de Cocoa
¼ Sweet Cream
Shake well
Strain into Cocktail Glass

Alexander Cocktail—No. 2

⅓ Crème de Cocoa
⅓ Brandy
⅓ Sweet Cream
Shake well
Strain into Cocktail Glass

Alfonso Cocktail

1 dash Angostura Bitters
4 dashes Italian Vermouth
¼ Dry Gin
¼ French Vermouth
½ Grand Marnier Liqueur
Shake well
Strain into Cocktail Glass

Allen Cocktail

1 dash Lemon Juice
⅓ Maraschino
⅔ Plymouth Gin
Shake well
Strain into Cocktail Glass

Allies Cocktail

½ Dry Gin
½ French Vermouth
2 dashes Kummel
Shake well
Strain into Cocktail Glass

Almond Cocktail

(Serves 6 people)
2 jiggers Gin (warmed)
1 teaspoon Powdered Sugar
6 peeled Almonds
Let mixture cool
Add 1 teaspoon Kirschwasser
1 teaspoon Peach Brandy
1 jigger French Vermouth
1 jigger Sauternes
Shake well with ice
Strain into Cocktail Glass

Alsace Lorraine Cocktail

¼ jigger Kirschwasser
¼ jigger Anisette
Pour into Pony Glass
Serve with Water Chaser

Amber Dawn Cocktail

½ Jamaica Rum
½ Orange Juice
1 dash Curacao
1 dash water
Shake well
Strain into Cocktail Glass

Amber Dream Cocktail

⅔ jigger Dry Gin
1 tablespoon Chartreuse
⅓ jigger Italian Vermouth
1 dash Orange Bitters
Shake well
Strain into Cocktail Glass

American Beauty Cocktail

1 dash Crème de Menthe
¼ Orange Juice
¼ Grenadine
¼ French Vermouth
¼ Cognac Brandy
Shake well
Strain into Medium Glass
Top with Port Wine

American Glory Cocktail

1 jigger Champagne
1 jigger Orange Juice
Serve in Medium Glass—stir gently
Fill with Soda—serve with straw

Amer Picon Cocktail

1 jigger Amer Picon
1 pony Grenadine
Serve in Cocktail Glass
Fill with Soda

Amour Cocktail

2 dashes Orange Bitters
½ jigger Sherry
½ jigger Italian Vermouth
Stir — serve in Cocktail Glass

Amsterdam Cocktail

½ Holland Gin
¼ Orange Juice
¼ Cointreau
4 dashes Orange Bitters
Shake well
Strain into Cocktail Glass
(A favorite at the Carlton Hotel,
   Amsterdam, Netherlands)

Angeles Cocktail

1 pony Dry Gin
1 dash Pernod's
3 dashes Grenadine
1 teaspoon Lime Juice
½ White of one Egg
1 sprinkle of Nutmeg
Shake well
Strain into Cocktail Glass
Serve in Pony Glass

Angel Face Cocktail

⅓ Dry Gin
⅓ Apricot Liqueur
⅓ Calvados
Shake — strain into Cocktail Glass

Angelic Cocktail

1 pony Whiskey
1/6 jigger Grenadine
1/6 jigger Crème de Cocoa
1/6 jigger Cream
Shake well
Strain into Cocktail Glass
Grate Nutmeg over top

Angel's Dream Cocktail

⅓ Maraschino
⅓ Sweet Cream
⅓ Crème Yvette

Angel's Kiss Cocktail

¼ Crème de Cocoa
¼ Prunelle Liqueur
¼ Crème de Violette
¼ Sweet Cream
Pour in order into Liqueur Glass

Angel's Lips Cocktail

⅔ Benedictine
⅓ Sweet Cream
Serve in Pony Glass

Angel's Tip

⅔ Maraschino
⅓ Sweet Cream
Serve in Pony Glass
Pierce a Cherry with a toothpick
   and lay across top of glass

Angel's Wing Cocktail

⅓ Cherry Liqueur
⅓ Maraschino
⅓ Parfait Amour
Keep colors separate
Serve in Cocktail Glass

Anisette Cocktail—No. 1

1 pony Dry Gin
¼ jigger Anisette
¼ Sweet Cream
½ White of one Egg
Nutmeg to taste

Anisette Cocktail—No. 2

1 pony Pernod's
1 spoon Benedictine
1 dash Angostura Bitters
Shake well
Serve in Frosted Cocktail Glass
Drip mixture through water till full

Announcer Cocktail

⅛ Lemon Juice
⅛ Cointreau
⅜ Dry Gin
⅜ Cognac Brandy
Shake well
Serve in Cocktail Glass

Ante Cocktail

1 dash Angostura Bitters
¼ Pernod's
¼ Cointreau
¼ Calvados
Shake well
Strain into Cocktail Glass

Apértif Cocktail

½ Dry Gin
½ Dubonnet
Juice of ½ Orange
Stir well
Strain into Cocktail Glass

Apparent Cocktail

½ Dry Gin
½ Dubonnet
1 dash Pernod's
Stir well
Strain into Cocktail Glass

Apple Blossom Cocktail

⅔ jigger Applejack
⅓ jigger Italian Vermouth
2 dashes Grenadine
2 dashes Pineapple
Stir well
Serve in Cocktail Glass

Applejack Cocktail—No. 1

1 dash Angostura Bitters
½ Italian Vermouth
½ Calvados
Stir well
Strain into Cocktail Glass

Applejack Cocktail—No. 2

2/3 Applejack
1/6 Grenadine
1/6 Lemon Juice
Stir well
Serve in Cocktail Glass

Applejack Cocktail—No. 3

¾ jigger Applejack
1 spoon Lemon Juice
1 spoon Brandy
1 spoon Sugar Syrup
Shake
Strain into highball Glass
Fill with Seltzer

Apple Pie Cocktail

½ Cuban Rum
½ Italian Vermouth
4 dashes Apricot Liqueur
2 dashes Grenadine
4 dashes Lemon Juice
Stir well
Strain into Cocktail Glass

Apple Toddy

(Medium Glass)
Dissolve one lump of Sugar in 3
    teaspoons water
1 jigger Applejack
1 lump ice
Serve with spoon and sprinkle of
    Nutmeg

Apricot Cocktail

⅔ jigger Dry Gin
⅓ jigger Apricot Liqueur
5 drops Lime Juice
Stir well
Strain into Cocktail Glass

Astor Cocktail

1 dash Lemon Juice
1 dash Orange Juice
1 jigger Dry Gin
Stir and serve in Cocktail Glass

Atlas Cocktail

1 dash Angostura Bitters
¼ Cointreau
¼ Demerara Rum — 151 proof
½ Calvados
Stir well
Serve in Cocktail Glass

Atty Cocktail

¼ French Vermouth
3 dashes Pernod's
¾ Dry Gin
3 dashes Crème de Violette
Stir well
Strain into Cocktail Glass

Aviation Cocktail

⅓ Lemon Juice
⅔ Dry Gin
2 dashes Maraschino
Stir — strain into Cocktail Glass

Aviator Cocktail

1 pony Dubonnet
1 pony Sherry
Stir
Strain into Cocktail Glass
Twist Lemon Peel over top

Babbie's Special Cocktail

1 dash Dry Gin
⅓ Sweet Cream
⅔ Apricot Liqueur
Stir — strain into Cocktail Glass

Baby Fingers Cocktail

⅔ jigger Sloe Gin
⅓ jigger Dry Gin
2 dashes Angostura
Stir well
Strain into Cocktail Glass

Baby Kitty Cocktail

⅓ Anisette
⅓ Crème de Violette
⅓ Whipped Cream
Serve in Sherry Glass
Top with Cherry

Bacardi Cocktail—No. 1

1 jigger Bacardi Rum
Juice of one Lime
½ teaspoon Sugar
1 dash Grenadine
Shake well
Serve in Cocktail Glass

Bacardi Cocktail—No. 2

Juice of one Lime
½ spoon Sugar
1 jigger Bacardi
1 pony Pineapple Juice
Serve in Champagne Glass with
    shaved ice

Bacardi Buck Cocktail

1 jigger Bacardi Rum
1 pony Cointreau
2 spoons Lemon Juice
2 spoons Sugar Syrup
Shake well
Strain into Highball Glass
Fill with Lime Rickey

Bacardi Dubonnet

⅓ jigger Bacardi
⅓ jigger Dubonnet
1 spoon Grenadine
1 spoon Lime Juice
Stir with ice
Strain into Cocktail Glass

Bacardi Peach Cocktail

⅓ jigger Bacardi
1 spoon Lemon Juice
⅓ jigger Peach Brandy
1 spoon Sugar Syrup
1 Sprig Mint
Shake well
Strain into Cocktail Glass

Bacardi Vermouth

½ jigger Bacardi
½ jigger Vermouth
Stir well
Strain into Cocktail Glass

Ballantine Cocktail

2 dashes Orange Bitters
½ jigger French Vermouth
½ jigger Plymouth Gin
1 dash Pernod's
Stir well
Strain into Cocktail Glass

Balm Cocktail

½ glass Orange Juice
½ glass Cointreau
3 glasses Sherry
1 dash Orange Bitters
2 dashes Jamaica Rum
Stir well — serve in Cocktail Glass
    with Olive

Baltimore Cocktail

1 pony Cognac
¾ jigger Madeira
2 spoons Sugar Syrup
2 jiggers Milk
1 Egg
¼ jigger Rum
Shake well
Strain into Highball Glass
Grate Nutmeg over and serve

Barbara Cocktail—No. 1

¼ Sweet Cream
¼ Crème de Cocoa
½ Vodka
Stir well
Serve in Cocktail Glass

Barbara Cocktail—No. 2

⅔ jigger Whiskey
⅓ jigger Grapefruit Juice
2 dashes Apricot Liqueur
1 dash Sugar Syrup
Shake well
Strain into Cocktail Glass

Barbary Coast Cocktail

¼ Dry Gin
¼ Scotch Whisky
¼ Crème de Cocoa
¼ Sweet Cream
Stir well
Strain into Highball Glass

Barnacle Bill Cocktail

⅓ Chartreuse
⅓ Parfait Amour
⅓ Pernod's
Stir well
Strain into Cocktail Glass

Barton Special Cocktail

¼ Calvados
¼ Scotch Whisky
½ Dry Gin
Stir well
Strain into Cocktail Glass

Battery Charger Cocktail

1 tablespoon Grenadine
1 pony Pernod's
½ glass Cracked Ice
Stir — fill with Seltzer

B and B Cocktail

½ Benedictine
½ Cognac Brandy
Serve in Pony Glass

Beau Brummel Cocktail

1 pony Whiskey
1 pony Orange Juice
2 dashes Prunelle
1 spoon Sugar Syrup
Stir well
Strain into Cocktail Glass

Beaux Arts Cocktail

1/3 jigger Dry Gin
1/6 jigger Italian Vermouth
1 spoon Pineapple
1/6 jigger French Vermouth
1 dash Anisette
1 spoon Orange Juice
Shake well
Strain into Cocktail Glass

Bebbo Cocktail

1 pony Lemon Juice
1 spoon Orange Juice
1 spoon Honey
1 jigger Dry Gin
Shake well
Strain into Cocktail Glass

Bee's Knees Cocktail

1 teaspoon Honey
⅓ Lemon Juice
⅔ Applejack
Shake well with ice
Serve in Cocktail Glass

Benedictine Cocktail

¼ Benedictine
¼ Lemon Juice
½ Cognac Brandy
Stir well
Strain into Cocktail Glass

Benedictine Frappé

Frappé Glass ⅔ full of ice
Benedictine to fill
Dress with Fruit
Serve with straw

Bently Cocktail

½ Calvados
½ Dubonnet
Shake well
Strain into Cocktail Glass

Bermudian Cocktail

⅓ jigger Dry Gin
¼ jigger Apricot Liqueur
¼ jigger Grenadine
1 spoon Lemon Juice
1 spoon Sugar Syrup
Shake well
Strain into Cocktail Glass

Berry Cocktail

1/6 Orange Juice
1/6 Pineapple Juice
2/3 Bacardi Rum
1 dash Grenadine
Shake well
Strain into Cocktail Glass

Betty Cocktail

⅓ jigger Dry Gin
⅓ Cointreau
⅓ jigger Bacardi Rum
Shake well
Strain into Cocktail Glass

Between the Sheets Cocktail

1 dash Lemon Juice
⅓ Brandy
⅓ Cointreau
⅓ Bacardi Rum
Shake well
Serve in Cocktail Glass

Biffy Cocktail

¼ Lemon Juice
¼ Swedish Punch
½ Dry Gin
Shake well
Serve in Cocktail Glass

Big Bad Wolf Cocktail

Yolk of one Egg
1 teaspoon Grenadine
⅓ Orange Curacao
⅔ Brandy
Shake well
Strain into Cocktail Glass

Bijou Cocktail—No. 1

⅔ jigger Dry Gin
⅓ Grand Marnier
Shake well
Strain into Cocktail Glass

Bijou Cocktail—No. 2

1 dash Amer Picon
⅓ Plymouth Gin
1 dash Orange Bitters
⅓ Green Chartreuse
⅓ Italian Vermouth
Shake well
Serve in Cocktail Glass
Add Cherry or Olive
Twist of Lemon Peel

Bim Cocktail

¾ jigger Barcardi
1 spoon Curacao
1 spoon Grenadine
1 spoon Pineapple Juice
1 spoon Orange Juice
Shake well
Strain into Cocktail Glass

Bimini Cocktail—No. 1

¾ jigger Bacardi Rum
1 spoon Curacao
1 spoon Grenadine
1 spoon Pineapple Juice
1 spoon Orange Juice
Stir well
Strain into Cocktail Glass

Bimini Cocktail—No. 2

1 jigger Crème de Cocoa
1 jigger Dry Gin
1 jigger Sweet Cream
2 lumps ice in Highball Glass
Fill glass with Seltzer

Bird Cocktail

(Use Bar Glass)
Twist two pieces of Orange Peel
Fill glass with fine ice
⅔ jigger Triple-Sec Curacao
⅓ jigger Cognac Brandy
Add two more twists of Orange Peel
Frappé and serve

Bishop Cocktail—No. 1

1 pony Whiskey
¼ jigger Italian Vermouth
¼ jigger Orange Juice
1 dash Chartreuse
Shake well
Strain into Cocktail Glass

Bishop Cocktail—No. 2

Juice of one Lime
½ barspoon Sugar
⅓ Claret
⅔ Bacardi Rum
Shake well
Strain into Cocktail Glass

Bishop Poker Cocktail

⅓ French Vermouth
⅓ Italian Vermouth
⅓ Plymouth Gin
1 dash Amer Picon Bitters
Shake well
Strain into Cocktail Glass

Biter Cocktail

(6 people)
3 jiggers Gin
1½ jiggers Lemon Juice
1½ jiggers Green Chartreuse
1 dash Pernod's
Shake well
Strain into Cocktail Glass

Black Jack Cocktail—No. 1

1 pony Dry Gin
¼ jigger Kirschwasser
¼ jigger Crème de Cassis
Stir well
Strain into Cocktail Glass
Add Cherry and Twist of Orange
    Peel

Black Jack Cocktail—No. 2

1 pony Kirschwasser
1 dash Brandy
1 pony Coffee
Stir — serve in Claret Glass

Black Stripe Cocktail

1½ jiggers Rum
2 spoons Honey
Dissolve Honey in hot water in
    Highball Glass — add ice, Rum
Stir well — fill with water
Grate Nutmeg over — serve

Blackthorne Cocktail — No. 1

⅓ jigger Sloe Gin
⅓ jigger French Vermouth
⅓ jigger Italian Vermouth
1 dash Orange Bitters
1 dash Angostura Bitters
Stir well
Strain into Cocktail Glass
Twist Lemon Peel on top

Blackthorne Cocktail — No. 2

1 pony Dry Gin
¼ jigger Dubonnet
¼ jigger Kirschwasser
Stir well
Strain into Cocktail Glass

Blackthorne Cocktail — No. 3

2 dashes Orange Bitters
⅓ Italian Vermouth
⅔ Sloe Gin
Stir — strain into Cocktail Glass

Blackthorne Cocktail — No. 4

2 dashes Angostura Bitters
3 dashes Pernod's
½ Irish Whiskey
½ French Vermouth
Shake well
Strain into Cocktail Glass

Black Velvet Cocktail

Use long Tumbler
½ Guinness Stout
½ Champagne
Do not stir

Blanche Cocktail

⅓ Cointreau
⅓ Anisette
⅓ Curacao Triple-Sec
Stir well
Strain into Cocktail Glass

Blarny Cocktail

⅓ Italian Vermouth
⅔ Irish Whiskey
Serve in Old Fashioned Glass
Dress with Fruit

Block and Tackle Cocktail

1/6 Pernod's
1/6 Calvados
1/3 Cointreau
1/3 Cognac
Stir well
Strain into Cocktail Glass

Blood and Sand Cocktail

¼ Orange Juice
¼ Scotch Whisky
¼ Cherry Brandy
¼ Italian Vermouth
Stir well
Strain into Cocktail Glass

Bloodhound Cocktail — No. 1

¼ French Vermouth
¼ Italian Vermouth
½ Dry Gin
3 crushed Strawberries
Shake well
Strain into Cocktail Glass

Bloodhound Cocktail — No. 2

⅓ jigger Dry Gin
⅓ jigger Italian Vermouth
⅓ jigger French Vermouth
1 dash Grenadine
6 crushed Raspberries
Shake well
Strain into Cocktail Glass

Blue Blazer Cocktail

1 lump Sugar
Dissolve in ¼ jigger hot water
1 jigger Scotch Whisky
Set fire to Whisky
Pour from one mug to the other
Sweeten with 1 spoon Powdered
  Sugar

Blue Monday Cocktail

¼ Cointreau
¾ Vodka
2 dashes Parfait Amour
Stir well
Strain into Cocktail Glass

Blue Moon Cocktail

⅓ Benedictine
⅓ Rye Whiskey
⅓ Ginger Ale
Shake well
Strain into Cocktail Glass

Blue Train Cocktail

¼ Lemon Juice
¼ Cointreau
¼ Dry Gin
¼ Crème de Violette
Shake well
Strain into Cocktail Glass

Boa Constrictor Cocktail

1 glass Blackberry Brandy
Shake well with ice
Strain into Cocktail Glass
Grate Nutmeg on top

Bobby Burns Cocktail

½ Italian Vermouth
½ Scotch Whisky
3 dashes Benedictine
Shake well
Strain into Cocktail Glass
Twist Lemon Peel on top

Bombay Cocktail

4 dashes Lemon Juice
¾ jigger East Indian Punch
Serve in Pimm's No. 1 Cup

Bonanza Cocktail

1 pony Brandy
1 jigger Sherry
Stir in Highball Glass
Fill with Riesling

Bonnie Prince Charlie Cocktail

⅓ Drambuie
⅔ Cognac
Juice of ½ Lime
Shake well
Strain into Cocktail Glass

Boomerang Cocktail

1 dash Lemon Juice
1 dash Angostura Bitters
⅓ French Vermouth
⅓ Bourbon
⅓ Swedish Punch
Shake well
Strain into Cocktail Glass

Booster Cocktail

4 dashes Curacao
White of one Egg
1 jigger Brandy
Shake well
Strain into Cocktail Glass
Grate Nutmeg on top

Bosom Cocktail

Yolk of one Egg
1 teaspoon Grenadine
⅓ Curacao
⅔ Cognac
Shake well
Strain into Cocktail Glass

Boston Club Cocktail

⅔ jigger Dry Gin
⅓ Italian Vermouth
Juice of ½ Lime
Shake well
Strain into Cocktail Glass

Boston Flip

1 pony Whiskey
1 pony Madeira
1 spoon Sugar Syrup
½ yolk of one Egg
Grate Nutmeg to taste
Shake well
Strain into Cocktail Glass

Bostonian Cocktail

2/3 jigger Dry Gin
1/6 Italian Vermouth
1/2 spoon Orange Juice
1/2 spoon Lemon Juice
1 scant spoon Sugar Syrup
3 sprigs Mint
Crush Mint with Fruit Juices and
    Syrup — add liquor
Shake well
Serve in Cocktail Glass

Boulevard Cocktail

⅓ Dry Gin
⅓ Italian Vermouth
⅓ Orange Juice
Shake well
Strain into Cocktail Glass

Boulevard Cocktail—No. 2

1 pony Pernod's
1 pony Italian Vermouth
2 drops Angostura Bitters
Stir well
Serve in Cocktail Glass
Twist Lemon Peel over top

88

Brainstorm Cocktail

½ jigger Irish Whiskey
2 dashes Benedictine
2 dashes French Vermouth
Squeeze Orange Peel on top
Stir well
Strain into Cocktail Glass

Brandy Champerelle

Use small Wine Glass
⅓ Orange Curacao
⅓ Cognac Brandy
3 drops Angostura

Brandy Cocktail—No. 1

1 dash Angostura Bitters
1 dash Dry Gin
1 jigger Cognac Brandy
Stir — serve in Cocktail Glass

Brandy Cocktail—No. 2

1 jigger Cognac
2 dashes Gomme Syrup
2 drops Angostura Bitters
Stir well
Strain into Cocktail Glass

Brandy Cocktail—No. 3

1 jigger Cognac
2 dashes Curacao
1 dash Angostura
Stir well
Strain into Cocktail Glass
Add Olive

Brandy Crusta

Use Bar Glass with shaved ice
Add 4 dashes Gomme Syrup
2 dashes Angostura Bitters
2 dashes Lemon Juice
2 dashes Maraschino
1 jigger Cognac
Stir — strain into glass containing whole rind of one Lemon coated with Powdered Sugar—then dress with fruits in season

Brandy Daisy

4 dashes Gomme Syrup
3 dashes Curacao
Juice of ½ Lemon
1 jigger Brandy
Shake well
Strain into Medium Glass ¾ full of ice
Serve with Seltzer

Brandy Gomme

3 dashes Gomme Syrup
2 dashes Curacao
1 iigger Cognac Brandy
Stir
Strain into Cocktail Glass
Twist Lemon Peel on top

Brandy Scaffa

⅓ Maraschino
⅓ Green Chartreuse
⅓ Cognac
Keep ingredients separate in Pony Glass

Brazil Cocktail

⅓ jigger Sherry
2 dashes Pernod's
⅓ jigger French Vermouth
1 dash Orange Bitters
2 dashes Sugar Syrup
Stir well
Strain into Cocktail Glass

Broadway Smile

⅓ Crème de Cassis
⅓ Swedish Punch
⅓ Cointreau
Keep colors separate in Liqueur
   Glass

Broken Spur Cocktail

Yolk of one Egg
1/6 Dry Gin
1/6 Italian Vermouth
2/3 White Port
1 teaspoon Anisette
Shake well
Strain into Cocktail Glass

Broker Cocktail

1 pony White Port
1 spoon Italian Vermouth
1 spoon Dry Gin
1 dash Anisette
½ yolk of one Egg
Shake well
Strain into Cocktail Glass

Bronx Cocktail — No. 2

¼ Italian Vermouth
¼ French Vermouth
½ Dry Gin
Piece of Orange Peel
Stir well
Strain into Cocktail Glass

Bronx Cocktail–(Original)

⅔ Dry Gin
⅓ Orange Juice
1 dash French Vermouth
1 dash Italian Vermouth
Stir
Strain into Cocktail Glass

Bronx Terrace Cocktail

⅔ Dry Gin
⅓ French Vermouth
Juice of ½ Lime
Stir well
Strain into Cocktail Glass

Brooklyn Cocktail

1 dash Amer Picon
1 dash Maraschino
⅔ Whiskey
⅓ French Vermouth
Stir well
Strain into Cocktail Glass

Brown University Cocktail

½ French Vermouth
½ Whiskey
2 dashes Orange Bitters
Stir well
Strain into Cocktail Glass

Brunelle Cocktail

¼ Pernod's
½ tablespoon Sugar
¾ Lemon Juice
Shake well
Strain into Cocktail Glass

Brut Cocktail

⅔ jigger French Vermouth
⅓ jigger Amer Picon
2 dashes Orange Bitters
3 drops Angostura
Stir well
Strain into Cocktail Glass
Twist Lemon Peel on top

Bud's Special Cocktail

1 dash Angostura Bitters
⅓ Sweet Cream
⅔ Cointreau
Stir well
Strain into Cocktail Glass

Builder Upper Cocktail

Juice of one Lemon
1 ounce Benedictine
1 jigger Cognac
Place whole rind of Lemon in
    Collins Glass — add ice and
    liquor — fill with Soda

Bumper Cocktail

⅔ jigger Jamaica Rum
⅓ jigger Dry Gin
1 dash Lemon Juice
Stir well
Strain into Cocktail Glass
Twist Lemon Peel over top

Bunny Hug Cocktail–No. 1

⅓ Dry Gin
⅓ Whiskey
⅓ Pernod's
Shake well
Strain in Cocktail Glass

Bunny Hug Cocktail–No. 2

⅓ Dry Gin
⅓ Scotch Whisky
⅓ Pernod's
1 dash Anisette
Shake well
Strain into Cocktail Glass

Burnt Brandy and Peach Cocktail

1 jigger Cognac
2 lumps Sugar
Burn Brandy with Sugar in saucer
2 or 3 pieces of Fresh Peach
Place Fruit in glass
Pour in the burnt liquid and serve

Bustanobee Cocktail

⅔ jigger Crème de Menthe
1 spoon Sugar Syrup
1 dash Angostura Bitters
2 spoons Orange Juice
Shake well
Strain into Cocktail Glass

Byculla Cocktail

1 pony Ginger
1 pony Curacao
1 pony Port
1 pony Sherry
Shake well
Strain into Cocktail Glass

Cafe Bruler Cocktail

Moisten edge of Claret Glass
Dip glass into Powdered Sugar
⅞ Hot Coffee
⅛ Cognac Brandy
Set fire to Brandy

Cafe De Paris

White of one Egg
3 dashes Anisette
1 teaspoon Cream
1 jigger Dry Gin
Shake well
Strain into Cocktail Glass

Café Kirsch Cocktail

White of one Egg
¼ spoon Sugar
1 pony Cognac
1 pony Kirschwasser
1 pony Coffee
Shake well
Strain into Claret Glass
May be served hot or cold

Caliente Cocktail

1 pony Dry Gin
1 spoon Lemon Juice
1 spoon Sugar Syrup
1 spoon Sweet Cream
½ White of one Egg
Shake well
Strain into Cocktail Glass
Grate Nutmeg over top

Calvados Cocktail—No. 1

¼ Italian Vermouth
¼ Calvados
½ Brandy
Stir well
Strain into Cocktail Glass

Calvados Cocktail—No. 2

1 jigger Calvados
2 dashes Curacao
2 dashes Sugar Syrup
Shake well
Strain into Cocktail Glass

Calvados Cocktail—No. 3

(6 people)
2 jiggers Calvados
2 jiggers Orange Juice
1 jigger Cointreau
1 jigger Orange Bitters
Shake well
Strain into Cocktail Glass

Cameron's Kick Cocktail

1/3 Scotch Whisky
1/3 Irish Whiskey
1/6 Lemon Juice
1/6 Orgeat Syrup
Shake well
Strain into Cocktail Glass

Canadian Cocktail

¾ jigger Whiskey
1 dash Angostura
2 dashes Curacao
1 spoon Sugar Syrup
Shake well
Strain into Cocktail Glass
Twist Lemon Peel over top

Caprice Cocktail

⅔ jigger Dry Gin
1 spoon French Vermouth
1 spoon Benedictine
2 dashes Orange Bitters
Shake well
Strain into Cocktail Glass
Add a ripe Olive

Carlton Cocktail

½ Canadian Bourbon
¼ Orange Juice
¼ Cointreau
Shake well
Strain into Cocktail Glass
(Made at the Bar of the Famous
   Carlton Hotel, Amsterdam,
      Netherlands.)

Carlton Special

⅓ Benedictine
⅓ Orange Bitters
⅓ Crème de Cocoa
Shake well
Strain into Cocktail Glass
(Made at the Carlton Hotel,
   Amsterdam, Netherlands.)

Carrol Cocktail

⅔ Cognac
⅓ Italian Vermouth
Stir well
Strain into Cocktail Glass
Serve with Pickled Onion

Caruso Cocktail

⅓ Dry Gin
⅓ French Vermouth
⅓ Green Crème de Menthe
Shake well
Strain into Cocktail Glass

Casino Cocktail—No. 1

⅓ Jigger Dry Gin
⅓ jigger Applejack
1/6 jigger Plum Brandy
1/6 jigger Italian Vermouth
1 dash Cointreau
Shake well
Strain into Cocktail Glass

Casino Cocktail—No. 2

2 dashes Maraschino
2 dashes Orange Bitters
2 dashes Lemon Juice
1 jigger Old Tom Gin
Stir well
Serve with Cherry

Cason Cocktail

1/6 Grenadine
1/6 Swedish Punch
1/6 Calvados
1/6 Lemon Juice
1/3 Dry Gin
Shake well
Strain into Cocktail Glass

Cassis Cocktail

1 pony Whiskey
¼ jigger French Vermouth
2 spoons Crème de Cassis
Shake well
Strain into Cocktail Glass
Add Cherry

Castle Dip Cocktail

½ Apple Jack
½ White Crème de Menthe
3 dashes Pernod's
Shake well
Serve in Cocktail Glass

Caterpillar Cocktail

⅔ jigger Whiskey
⅓ jigger Grape Juice
1 dash Angostura
Shake well
Strain into Cocktail Glass

Cat's Eye Cocktail

(6 People)
½ jigger Lemonade
½ jigger Water
2 jiggers Dry Gin
1 spoon Kirschwasser
½ jigger Cointreau
2 jiggers French Vermouth
Shake well
Strain into Cocktail Glass
Serve with Olive

Champagne Buck

1 pony Champagne
¼ jigger Dry Gin
2 dashes Cherry Brandy
1 spoon Orange Juice
Stir well with ice
Strain into Cocktail Glass

Champagne Cocktail–No. 1

1 lump Sugar in Champagne Glass
2 dashes Angostura Bitters
1 piece of Lemon Peel twisted
Fill glass with chilled Champagne

Champagne Cocktail–No. 2

1 lump Sugar
2 dashes Angostura Bitters
Fill Champagne Goblet ⅓ with ice
2 slices of Orange
Fill with chilled Champagne

Champagne du Marco

1 Liqueur Glass Ice Cream
2 dashes Maraschino
4 dashes Orange Curaco
2 dashes Cognac
Stir well in Medium Glass
Fill with chilled Champagne
Dress with Fruits in season

Champagne Flip

1 jigger Champagne
1 spoon Sugar Syrup
1 dash Brandy
½ yolk of one Egg
Shake Egg and Syrup well in ice
Pour in Champagne — strain
Dash with Brandy

Champagne Velvet

½ Champagne
½ Dublin Stout
Pour very carefully

Champs Elysées Cocktail

(6 People)
3 jiggers Cognac
1 jigger Chartreuse
½ jigger Lemon Juice
1 dash Angostura
Shake well
Strain into Cocktail Glass

Charleston Cocktail–No. 1

⅓ Bacardi
⅓ Dubonnet
⅓ Dry Gin
Shake well
Strain into Cocktail Glass

Charleston Cocktail–No. 2

1/6 Dry Gin
1/6 Kirschwasser
1/6 Maraschino
1/6 Curacao
1/6 Italian Vermouth
1/6 French Vermouth
Shake well
Strain into Cocktail Glass
Twist Lemon Peel on top

Charlie O Cocktail

⅔ jigger Dry Gin
⅓ jigger French Vermouth
1 dash Cointreau
1 dash Grand Marnier
Shake well
Strain into Cocktail Glass
Twist Lemon Peel over top

Chartreuse Cocktail

1 pony Whiskey
1/3 jigger Chartreuse
1/6 French Vermouth
Stir — serve with Cherry

Cheerio Cocktail

1 pony Whiskey
1 pony Curacao
1 dash Maraschino
Stir
Strain into Cocktail Glass

Cherry Cocktail

1 pony Cherry Liqueur
1 pony French Vermouth
1 dash Orange Bitters
Shake well
Strain into Cocktail Glass
Add Cherry and serve

Cherry Blossom Cocktail —No. 1

¾ jigger Dry Gin
2 dashes Raspberry
2 dashes Orange Bitters
½ white of one Egg
Shake well
Strain into Cocktail Glass
Grate Nutmeg over top

Cherry Blossom Cocktail —No. 2

(6 People)
1 tablespoon Curacao
1 tablespoon Lemon Juice
1 tablespoon Grenadine
2½ jiggers Cherry Brandy
2 jiggers Cognac Brandy
Shake well
Serve very cold

Chevalier Cocktail

⅓ jigger Brandy
1 dash Angostura
1 dash Cointreau
⅓ jigger Lemon Juice
2 spoons Sugar Syrup
Shake well
Strain into Cocktail Glass

Chicago Cocktail

⅔ jigger Brandy
3 dashes Champagne
2 dashes Curacao
1 dash Angostura
Stir all except Champagne
Strain into Frosted Cocktail Glass
Add Twisted Lemon Peel and
    Champagne

Chinese Cocktail

2 dashes Angostura
3 dashes Maraschino
3 dashes Curacao
3 dashes Grenadine
⅔ jigger Jamaica Rum
Shake well
Strain into Cocktail Glass
Add Cherry
Twist Lemon on top

Chocolate Cocktail—No. 1

1 teaspoon Powdered Sugar
1 Egg
1 pony Maraschino
1 pony Chartreuse
1 teaspoon crushed Chocolate
Shake well
Strain into a Large Glass

Chocolate Cocktail—No. 2

Yolk of one Egg
¼ Chartreuse
¾ Port Wine
1 teaspoon crushed Chocolate
Shake well
Serve in a Medium Glass

Chocolate Soldier Cocktail

⅓ Dubonnet
⅔ Dry Gin
1 dash Lime Juice
Stir — serve in Cocktail Glass

Choker Cocktail

2 jiggers Scotch Whisky
1 jigger Pernod's
1 dash Angostura Bitters
Shake well
Strain into Cocktail Glass

Chrysanthemum Cocktail

3 dashes Pernod's
⅓ Benedictine
⅔ French Vermouth
Shake well
Strain into Cocktail Glass

Claridge Cocktail

1/3 Dry Gin
⅓ French Vermouth
1/6 Apricot Brandy
1/6 Cointreau
Shake well
Strain into Cocktail Glass

Classic Cocktail

1/6 Lemon Juice
1/6 Curacao
1/6 Maraschino
1/6 Brandy
Shake well
Strain into Cocktail Glass
Frost rim of glass with Powdered
    Sugar
Twist Lemon over top

Climax Cocktail

⅓ jigger Applejack
⅓ jigger French Vermouth
1 spoon Lime Juice
1 spoon Grenadine
½ white of one egg
Shake well
Strain into Cocktail Glass
Grate Nutmeg over top

Clover Club Cocktail—No. 1

Juice of ½ Lime
½ spoon Sugar
½ pony Raspberry Syrup
¼ pony white of Egg
1 jigger Dry Gin
Shake well
Strain into Cocktail Glass

Clover Club Cocktail—No. 2

¾ jigger Dry Gin
1 spoon Grenadine
4 drops Lemon Juice
½ white of one Egg
Shake well
Strain into Cocktail Glass
Grate Nutmeg over top

Clover Leaf Cocktail

1 pony Dry Gin
1 spoon Lemon Juice
½ white of one Egg
¼ jigger French Vermouth
1 spoon Grenadine
Sprig of Mint
Bruise Mint
Shake well with ice
Strain into Cocktail Glass
Decorate

Club Forest Cocktail

⅓ jigger Port
⅓ jigger Chartreuse
½ yolk of one Egg
½ spoon Sugar Syrup
1 spoon Curacao
Shake well
Strain into Cocktail Glass
Grate Nutmeg over top

Cockney Cocktail

1 pony Dry Gin
1 pony Champagne
1 spoon Lemon Juice
½ spoon Sugar Syrup
Stir
Strain into Cocktail Glass

Coffee Cocktail—No. 1

⅓ jigger Brandy
⅓ jigger Coffee
⅓ jigger Cointreau
Shake well
Strain into Cocktail Glass

Coffee Cocktail—No. 2

⅓ jigger Brandy
⅓ jigger Port
½ Egg
½ spoon Sugar
Shake well
Strain into Cocktail Glass
Grate Nutmeg over top

Coffee Cocktail—No. 3

1 jigger Port
1 pony Crème de Cocoa
1 dash Brandy
½ yolk of one Egg
Shake well
Strain into Cocktail Glass
Grate Nutmeg over top

Coffee Cocktail—No. 4

1 jigger Port Wine
1 pony Brandy
Yolk of one Egg
½ spoon Bar Sugar
Shake well
Strain into Claret Glass

Cognac Cocktail

1 pony Brandy
1 pony Lemon Juice
1 dash Cointreau
1 dash Orange Bitters
Stir — strain into Cocktail Glass
Twist Lemon Peel over glass

Cointreau Cocktail

⅓ jigger Dry Gin
⅓ jigger Bacardi Rum
⅓ jigger Cointreau
Shake well
Strain into Cocktail Glass

Cola Absent

¼ glass Shaved Ice
2 tablespoons Pernod's
Fill with Coca Cola
Stir gently

Cola Cocktail

⅓ Dry Gin
⅔ Orange Curacao
2 dashes Orange Bitters
Shake well
Strain into Cocktail Glass

Cold Deck Cocktail

¼ White Crème de Menthe
¼ Italian Vermouth
½ Brandy
Shake well
Strain into Cocktail Glass

Colonel Cocktail

2/3 jigger Whiskey
1/6 jigger Apricot
1 spoon Grapefruit Juice
1/2 spoon Sugar Syrup
Stir well
Strain into Cocktail Glass
Twist Lemon Peel over top

Colony Cocktail

⅓ Vermouth — French
⅔ Dry Gin
1 spoon Liqueur d'Or
3 dashes Orange Bitters
Shake well
Strain into Cocktail Glass

Commodore Cocktail —No. 1

½ teaspoon Sugar
1 dash Lemon Juice
White of one Egg
1 jigger Bacardi Rum
1 dash Grenadine
1 dash Raspberry Syrup
Shake well
Strain into Cocktail Glass

Commodore Cocktail No. 2

⅓ Lemon Juice
⅓ Bourbon
⅓ Crème de Cocoa
1 dash Grenadine
Shake well
Serve in Champagne Glass

Coral Cocktail

⅔ jigger Dry Gin
⅓ Italian Vermouth
1 spoon 7 Fruits
Shake well
Strain into Cocktail Glass

Coronation Cocktail—No. 1

⅓ Italian Vermouth
⅓ French Vermouth
⅓ Applejack
1 dash Peach Liqueur
Shake well
Strain into Cocktail Glass

Coronation Cocktail—No. 2

½ Sherry
½ French Vermouth
1 dash Maraschino
2 dashes Orange Bitters
Shake well
Strain into Cocktail Glass

Coronation Cocktail—No. 3

1 dash Peppermint
1 dash Peach Liqueur
3 dashes Curacao
⅔ jigger Brandy
Shake well
Strain into Cocktail Glass

Country Cocktail

⅓ jigger Applejack
1 spoon Lemon Juice
½ of whole Egg
⅓ jigger Port
1 spoon Sugar Syrup
Shake well
Strain into Cocktail Glass
Grate Nutmeg over

Country Gentleman Cocktail

1 pony Applejack
¼ jigger Curacao
1 spoon Lemon Juice
1 spoon Sugar Syrup
Shake well
Strain into Cocktail Glass

Cowboy Cocktail

⅔ Whiskey
⅓ Sweet Cream
Shake well
Strain into Cocktail Glass

Creole Cocktail—No. 1

¾ jigger Whiskey
1 dash Curacao
1 dash Angostura Bitters
1 dash Peychaud's Bitters
Wet glass with Pernod's
Stir well
Serve with Chaser

Creole Cocktail—No. 2

⅓ jigger Dry Gin
⅓ jigger Sherry
⅓ jigger Lemon Juice
Shake well
Strain into Cocktail Glass

Creole Cocktail—No. 3

1 dash Orange Bitters
⅓ jigger Pernod's
⅓ jigger Italian Vermouth
Shake well
Strain into Cocktail Glass

Creole Lady Cocktail

2 Maraschino Cherries
1 pony Maraschino
1 Sherry Glass Bourbon
1 Sherry Glass Madeira
Mix with spoon — no ice

Crook Cocktail

1 dash Orange Bitters
⅓ Pernod's
⅔ Italian Vermouth
Shake well
Strain into Cocktail Glass

Crux Cocktail

¼ Lemon Juice
¼ Cointreau
¼ Dubonnet
¼ Cognac
Shake well
Strain into Cocktail Glass

Cuba Libre Cocktail

½ Cuban Rum
½ Coca Cola
Juice of ½ Lime
Stir with ice

Cuban Cocktail—No. 1

⅔ jigger Bacardi Rum
⅓ jigger Lime Juice
Shake well
Strain into Cocktail Glass

Cuban Cocktail—No. 2

Juice of ½ Lime
⅓ Apricot Brandy
⅔ Bacardi Rum
Shake well
Strain into Cocktail Glass

Culross Cocktail

Juice of ¼ Lemon
⅓ Lillet
⅓ Bacardi Rum
⅓ Apricot Brandy
Shake well
Strain into Cocktail Glass

Cupid Cocktail

1 jigger Sherry
1 fresh Egg
1 teaspoon Powdered Sugar
1 dash Pepper
Shake well
Strain into Cocktail Glass

Curacao Cocktail

1 pony Whisky
1 pony Curacao
1 dash Lemon Juice
Shake well
Strain into Cocktail Glass

Curacao Cocktail

(6 People)
½ jigger Brandy
2½ jiggers Orange Curacao
2½ jiggers Orange Juice
½ jigger Dry Gin
Shake
Strain into glasses rinsed out with
    Orange Bitters

Daiquiri Cocktail

Juice of ½ Lime
1 teaspoon Powdered Sugar
1 jigger Cuban Rum — White
Shake well
Strain into Cocktail Glass

Dandy Cocktail

½ jigger Whiskey
½ jigger Dubonnet
1 dash Angostura Bitters
3 dashes Cointreau
1 piece Lemon Peel
1 piece Orange Peel
Shake well
Strain into Cocktail Glass

Darb Cocktail

⅓ French Vermouth
⅓ Dry Gin
⅓ Apricot Brandy
4 dashes Lemon Juice
Shake well
Strain into Cocktail Glass

Dare Devil Cocktail

⅔ jigger Port
¼ oz. — one Egg
1 dash Angostura Bitters
Shake well
Strain into Cocktail Glass

Davis Cocktail

¼ Jamaica Rum
½ French Vermouth
¼ Lime Juice
1 dash Grenadine
Shake well
Strain into Cocktail Glass

Deauville Cocktail

¼ Brandy
¼ Calvados
¼ Cointreau
¼ Lemon Juice
Shake well
Strain into Cocktail Glass

Delys Cocktail

⅓ jigger Dry Gin
⅓ Crème de Menthe
⅓ Crème de Violette
Shake well
Strain into Cocktail Glass

Demeanor Cocktail

1 dash Orange Bitters
½ jigger Old Tom Gin
½ jigger Italian Vermouth
2 dashes Crème de Violette
Stir — strain into Cocktail Glass

Dempsey Cocktail

2 dashes Pernod's
2 dashes Grenadine
½ jigger Dry Gin
½ jigger Calvados
Shake well
Strain into Cocktail Glass

Depth Bomb Cocktail

1 dash Lemon Juice
4 dashes Grenadine
½ jigger Calvados
½ jigger Brandy
Shake well
Strain into Cocktail Glass

Depth Charge Cocktail

2 dashes Pernod's
½ jigger Lillet
½ glass Dry Gin
Squeeze Orange Peel on top
Shake well
Strain into Cocktail Glass

de Rigueur Cocktail

½ jigger Whiskey
¼ jigger Grape Fruit Juice
¼ jigger Honey
Shake well
Strain into Cocktail Glass

Descent Cocktail—No. 1

1 jigger Brandy
½ jigger Port Wine
1 jigger Blackberry Brandy
1 teaspoon fine Sugar
½ barspoon ground Nutmeg
½ barspoon Jamaica Ginger
Stir well — without ice

Descent Cocktail—No. 2

1 jigger Blackberry Brandy
1 jigger Cognac Brandy
1 dash ground Nutmeg
Serve in Claret Glass — no ice

Desert Healer Cocktail

Juice of one Orange
1 jigger Dry Gin
1 pony Cherry Brandy
Shake — strain
Fill with Ginger Beer

Devil Cocktail

1 pony Brandy
1 pony Crème de Menthe
1 pinch Red Pepper
Shake well
Strain into Cocktail Glass
Sprinkle Red Pepper over top

Devil's Cocktail

½ Port Wine
½ French Vermouth
2 dashes Lemon Juice
Shake well
Strain into Cocktail Glass

Diabola Cocktail

⅔ Dubonnet
⅓ Dry Gin
2 dashes Orgeat Syrup
Shake well
Strain into Cocktail Glass

Diana Cocktail

Use Port Wine Glass
Add:
¾ White Crème de Menthe
¼ Cognac Brandy

Diki-Diki Cocktail—No. 1

1/6 Grapefruit Juice
1/6 Swedish Punch
2/3 Calvados Brandy
Shake well
Strain into Cocktail Glass

Diki-Diki Cocktail—No. 2

1 pony Calvados
¼ jigger Caloric Punch
¼ jigger Grape Fruit Juice
Shake well
Strain into Cocktail Glass

Dixie Cocktail

½ jigger Dry Gin
¼ jigger French Vermouth
¼ jigger Pernod's
Shake well
Strain into Cocktail Glass

Dizzy Cocktail

⅓ Whiskey
⅓ Sherry
⅓ Pineapple Juice
2 dashes Lemon Juice
Shake well
Strain into Cocktail Glass

Doctor Cocktail

½ jigger Lime Juice
½ jigger Swedish Punch
Shake well
Strain into Cocktail Glass

"Dodo" Cocktail

½ Dry Gin
½ Green Crème de Menthe
1 dash Lemon Juice
Shake well and
Strain into Cocktail Glass

Dolores Cocktail

½ Sherry
¼ Jamaica Rum
⅛ Dubonnet
⅛ Orange Juice
Shake well
Strain into Cocktail Glass

Donald H. Cocktail

1 dash Orange Bitters
⅓ Pernod's
⅔ Plymouth Gin
Stir well
Strain into Cocktail Glass

Dorothy's Delight Cocktail

⅓ French Vermouth
⅔ Old Tom Gin
Stir well
Strain into Cocktail Glass
Squeeze Orange and Lemon Peel on
    top

Double Rainbow

(6 People)
½ jigger Southern Comfort
3 jiggers Orange Juice
1 jigger Lemon Juice
1 pony Grenadine
Shake well
Strain into Cocktail Glass

Dream Cocktail—No. 1

⅓ Curacao
⅔ Brandy
1 dash Pernod's
Shake well
Strain into Cocktail Glass

Dream Cocktail—No. 2

1 pony Dry Gin
¼ jigger Apricot
¼ jigger Grenadine
1 dash Lemon Juice
Shake well
Strain into Cocktail Glass

Dubonnet Cocktail—No. 1

½ Dry Gin
½ Dubonnet
Stir well
Strain into Cocktail Glass

Dubonnet Cocktail—No. 2

1 pony Dry Gin
1 pony Dubonnet
2 dashes Maraschino
2 drops French Vermouth
Stir well
Strain into Cocktail Glass

Duchess Cocktail

1 dash Orange Bitters
⅓ Pernod's
⅓ French Vermouth
⅓ Italian Vermouth
Stir well
Strain into Cocktail Glass

Duck Under Cocktail

½ Dry Gin
½ Cointreau
1 dash Grape Juice
Stir well
Strain into Cocktail Glass

Dunlop Cocktail

1 dash Angostura Bitters
⅓ Sherry
⅔ Rum
Stir well
Strain into Cocktail Glass

Eagle's Dream Cocktail

1 teaspoon Powdered Sugar
White of one Egg
Juice of ¼ Lemon
¼ Parfait Amour
¾ Dry Gin
Shake well
Strain into Medium Glass

Earth-Quake Cocktail

⅓ Dry Gin
⅓ Whiskey
⅓ Pernod's
Shake well
Strain into Cocktail Glass

East and West Cocktail

1 dash Lemon Juice
¼ Bacardi Rum
¾ East India Punch
Shake well
Strain into Cocktail Glass

East India Cocktail

1 teaspoon Raspberry Syrup
1 teaspoon Red Curacao
3 dashes Angostura Bitters
3 dashes Maraschino
1 jigger Brandy
Stir well
Strain into Cocktail Glass
Twist Lemon Peel over top

Egg Nog

½ spoon Sugar
1 Egg
¾ jigger Milk
1 jigger Rum or Brandy
Shake well
Strain into Goblet
Grate Nutmeg on top

Elephant's Ear Cocktail

⅓ French Vermouth
⅓ Dry Gin
⅓ Dubonnet
Shake well
Strain into Cocktail Glass

Elixir Cocktail

⅔ Bacardi Elixir Cordial
⅓ Bacardi Rum
Juice of ½ Lime
½ bar spoon Sugar

Elk Cocktail

½ Prunelle Liqueur
2 dashes French Vermouth
½ Dry Gin
Shake well
Strain into Cocktail Glass

Emerald Cocktail

1 pony Cognac
1 pony Crème de Menthe, Green
1 dash Orange Bitters
Shake well
Strain into Cocktail Glass

Emergency Cocktail

⅔ jigger Gin
1 jigger Orange Ice
Shake well
Strain into Cocktail Glass
Grate Nutmeg over top

Emerson Cocktail

Juice of one Lime
½ teaspoon Maraschino
⅓ Old Tom Gin
⅓ Italian Vermouth
Stir well
Strain into Cocktail Glass

Empire Cocktail

¼ Apricot Brandy
¼ Calvados
½ Dry Gin
Shake well
Strain into Cocktail Glass

Erin Cocktail

⅔ jigger Dry Gin
⅓ jigger Green Crème de Menthe
Shake well
Strain into Cocktail Glass
Add a Green Olive

Erin's Irish Cocktail

3 dashes Green Crème de Menthe
6 dashes Green Chartreuse
1 jigger Irish Whiskey
Shake well
Strain into Cocktail Glass

Ethel Cocktail

⅓ Apricot Brandy
⅓ White Crème de Menthe
⅓ Curacao
Shake well
Strain into Cocktail Glass

Exposition Cocktail

⅓ Sloe Gin
⅓ Cherry Brandy
⅓ French Vermouth
Shake well
Strain into Cocktail Glass

Express Cocktail

1 dash Orange Bitters
½ Italian Vermouth
½ Scotch Whisky
Stir well
Strain into Cocktail Glass

Eye Opener Cocktail —No. 1

Yolk of one Egg
1 teaspoon Powdered Sugar
2 dashes Pernod's
2 dashes Curacao
1 pony Bacardi Rum
Shake well
Strain into Cocktail Glass

Eye Opener Cocktail —No. 2

Yolk of one fresh Egg
1 teaspoon Powdered Sugar
2 dashes Pernod's
2 dashes Curacao
2 dashes Crème de Noyaux
1 pony Jamaica Rum
Shake well
Strain into Cocktail Glass

Fair and Warmer Cocktail

⅓ Italian Vermouth
⅔ Cuban Rum
2 dashes Curacao
Shake well
Strain into Cocktail Glass

Fairy Belle Cocktail

White of one Egg
1 teaspoon Grenadine
¼ Apricot Liqueur
¾ Dry Gin
Shake well
Strain into Cocktail Glass

Fantasio Cocktail

1/6 White Crème de Menthe
1/6 Maraschino
1/3 Brandy
1/3 Dry Gin
Shake well
Strain into Cocktail Glass

Fascination Cocktail

⅓ Cointreau
⅔ Pernod's
1 piece ice in Champagne Glass
Fill from siphon

Favorite Cocktail

⅓ Cognac
⅔ Port
Stir
Strain into Cocktail Glass

Fedora Cocktail

1 pony Cognac
1 pony Curacao
½ pony Jamaica Rum
½ pony Bourbon
1 tablespoon Sugar dissolved in a
    little water
1 slice of Lemon
Shake well
Serve with Fruit in Glass filled with
    ice

Fernet Cocktail

⅓ jigger Brandy
⅓ jigger Fernet Branca
2 dashes Sugar Syrup
1 dash Angostura
Stir well
Strain into Cocktail Glass
Twist Lemon Peel over top

Fernet Branca Cocktail

¼ Fernet Branca
¼ Italian Vermouth
½ Dry Gin
Shake well
Strain into Cocktail Glass

Fifth Avenue Cocktail

⅓ Crème de Cocoa
⅓ Apricot Liqueur
⅓ Sweet Cream
Keep colors separate in Liqueur
    Glass

Fin de Siècle Cocktail

1 dash Orange Bitters
1 dash Amer Picon
⅓ Italian Vermouth
⅔ Plymouth Gin
Stir well
Strain into Cocktail Glass

Fine and Dandy Cocktail

¼ Lemon Juice
¼ Cointreau
½ Plymouth Gin
Shake well
Strain into Cocktail Glass

Fioupe Cocktail

⅓ jigger Brandy
⅓ jigger Italian Vermouth
1 spoon Benedictine
Stir well
Strain into Cocktail Glass
Add Cherry

Fitchett Cocktail

1 pony Dry Gin
¼ jigger Benedictine
⅓ jigger Italian Vermouth
1 dash Orange Bitters
Shake well
Strain into Cocktail Glass
Add Olive

Five Fifteen Cocktail

⅓ Curacao
⅓ French Vermouth
⅓ Sweet Cream
Shake well
Strain into Cocktail Glass

Floater Cocktail

Fill Cocktail Glass with shaved ice
Add ¾ Imported Kummel
¼ Cognac Brandy

Florida Special Cocktail

⅓ jigger Dry Gin
⅔ Orange Juice
Shake well
Strain into Cocktail Glass

Floridian Cocktail

⅓ Dry Gin
⅓ Rum
⅓ Orange Juice
Shake well
Strain into Cocktail Glass

Flu Cocktail

Juice of ¼ Lemon
1 dash of Jamaica Ginger
1 teaspoon Rock Candy Syrup
1 teaspoon Ginger Brandy
1 jigger Whiskey
Shake well
Strain into Cocktail Glass

Four Flush Cocktail

1 dash Grenadine
¼ French Vermouth
¼ Swedish Punch
½ Bacardi Rum
Shake well
Strain into Cocktail Glass

Fourth Degree Cocktail

⅓ Italian Vermouth
⅔ Plymouth Gin
1 dash Pernod's
Shake well
Strain into Cocktail Glass

Francuilli Cocktail

¼ Fernet Branca
¼ Italian Vermouth
½ Bourbon Whiskey
Serve as Frappé

Frankenstein Cocktail

1/3 Dry Gn
1/3 French Vermouth
1/6 Apricot Liqueur
1/6 Cointreau
Shake well
Strain into Cocktail Glass

French Rose Cocktail

¼ Cherry Brandy
¼ Kirschwasser
½ Dry Gin
Stir well
Strain into Cocktail Glass

French "75" Cocktail

⅔ Dry Gin
Juice of ¼ Lemon
1 spoon Powdered Sugar
Pour into Tall Glass
Full of cracked ice
Fill with Champagne

Frisco Cocktail

⅔ jigger Whiskey
⅓ Benedictine
Stir well
Strain into Cocktail Glass
Twist Lemon Peel over top

Full House Cocktail

1 dash Angostura
⅓ Yellow Chartreuse
⅓ Benedictine
⅓ Applejack
Shake well
Strain into Cocktail Glass

Gangadine Cocktail

1 teaspoon Framboise
⅓ Pernod's
⅓ White Crème de Menthe
⅓ Dry Gin
Shake well
Strain into Cocktail Glass

Garden of Eden Cocktail

½ pony Crème de Violette
½ pony Apricot Liqueur
Serve in Pony Glass

Gigolo Cocktail

1 pony Parfait Amour
1 pony Sweet Cream
1 spoon Honey
Stir Honey with Cream—no ice
Add Liqueur and stir
Grate Nutmeg over and serve

Gin Cocktail

1 jigger Dry Gin
1 dash Lemon
2 dashes Orange Bitters
Stir well in Bar Glass
Twist Lemon Peel over top

Gin Buck Cocktail

2 jiggers Dry Gin
½ jigger Lemon Juice
Put Lemon Peel in Highball Glass
Add cube of ice and Gin
Fill with Ginger Ale and stir

Gin Side Car Cocktail

Rub rim of Cocktail Glass with
    Lemon—dip Glass in Powdered
    Sugar; into a Mixing Glass put:
⅓ Dry Gin
⅓ Cointreau
Juice of ½ Lime
White of one Egg
1 dash Benedictine
Shake well
Strain into Cocktail Glass

Glad Eye Cocktail—No. 1

⅓ Green Crème de Menthe
⅔ Pernod's
Shake well
Strain into Cocktail Glass

Glad Eye Cocktail—No. 2

⅔ jigger Pernod's
⅓ jigger Sugar Syrup
1 Sprig Mint
Bruise Mint
Shake well together
Serve in Frosted Cocktail Glass

Gloom Chaser Cocktail

¼ Lemon Juice
¼ Grenadine
¼ Grand Marnier
¼ Orange Curacao
Shake well
Strain into Cocktail Glass

Gloom Lifter Cocktail

Juice of ½ Lemon
½ teaspoon Brandy
1 jigger Irish Whiskey
White of one Egg
½ teaspoon Sugar
1 dash Raspberry Syrup
1 dash Grenadine
Shake well
Strain into Cocktail Glass

Gloriana Cocktail

⅔ Apricot Liqueur
⅓ Dry Gin
1 dash Lime Juice
Shake well
Strain into Cocktail Glass

Goat's Delight Cocktail

½ Kirschwasser
½ Brandy
1 dash Orgeat Syrup
1 spoon Cream
1 dash Pernod's
Shake well
Strain into Cocktail Glass

Goddess of Love Cocktail

¾ jigger Pernod's
¼ jigger Anisette
Stir well
Strain into Cocktail Glass

Golden Dawn Cocktail —No. 1

¼ Dry Gin
¼ Apricot Liqueur
¼ Calvados
¼ Orange Juice
Shake well
Strain into Cocktail Glass

Golden Dawn Cocktail —No. 2

¼ Bacardi
¼ Dry Gin
¼ Cointreau
¼ Orange Juice
Shake well
Strain into Cocktail Glass

Golden Gate Cocktail

¾ Orange Ice
¼ Dry Gin
Shake well—use no ice
Serve in Cocktail Glass

Golden Slipper Cocktail

½ Yellow Chartreuse
1 small Egg Yolk
½ Goldwasser
Shake well
Strain into Cocktail Glass

Good Fellow Cocktail

1 pony Brandy
1 pony Benedictine
1 dash Angostura
2 dashes Sugar Syrup
Shake well
Strain into Cocktail Glass
Twist Lemon Peel over top

Gradeal Special Cocktail

¼ Dry Gin
¼ Apricot Liqueur
½ Bacardi Rum
Shake well
Strain into Cocktail Glass

Grand Slam Cocktail—No. 1

¼ French Vermouth
¼ Italian Vermouth
½ Swedish Punch
Shake well
Strain into Cocktail Glass

Grand Slam Cocktail—No. 2

⅓ jigger Dry Gin
⅓ jigger Brandy
⅓ jigger Apricot Liqueur
1 spoon Lime Juice
Shake well
Strain into Cocktail Glass

Grasshopper Cocktail

1 pony Crème de Menthe
1 pony Crème de Cocoa
Float Cocoa on top
Serve in Cocktail Glass

Green Dragon Cocktail

⅛ Lemon Juice
⅛ Kummel
¼ Green Crème de Menthe
½ Dry Gin
1 dash Peach Liqueur
Shake well
Strain into Cocktail Glass

Green Eye Cocktail

¾ Lillet
¼ Green Crème de Menthe
4 dashes Orange Bitters
Shake well
Strain into Cocktail Glass
Serve with Cherry on toothpick

Green Orchid Cocktail

Use Large Glass
½ full shaved ice
3 teaspoons Green Crème de
    Menthe
2 tablespoons Pernod's
white of one Egg
Shake well
Strain into Glass
Fill with Seltzer

Hague Cocktail

1 pony Whiskey
1 pony Chartreuse
1 spoon French Vermouth
Stir well
Strain into Cocktail Glass
Add Maraschino Cherry

Half and Half Cocktail

½ English Porter
½ English Ale
Serve in Tall Glass

Happy Thought Cocktail

Equal parts in Claret Glass
Filled with shaved ice
Anisette
Crème de Cocoa
Cognac
Crème de Rose
Crème de Menthe
Crème de Violette

Hari Kari Cocktail

Fill a Brandy Glass
½ with Whiskey Sour
Then fill with Apolinaris Water
Dress with Fruits

Harmony Cocktail

(Bar Glass)
¾ jigger Brandy
1 spoon Strawberry Syrup
2 dashes Orange Bitters
1 dash Maraschino
Stir well
Serve with spoon

Hart's Delight Cocktail

⅔ Jamaica Rum
⅓ Italian Vermouth
1 dash Angostura
Shake well
Strain into Cocktail Glass
Serve with Maraschino Cherry

Harvard Cocktail

1 dash Orange Bitters
2/5 jigger Brandy
3/5 jigger Italian Vermouth
Stir well
Strain into Highball Glass
Fill from siphon

Havana Cocktail—No. 1

1 pony Bacardi Rum
1 pony Sherry
1 dash Lemon Juice
Shake well
Strain into Cocktail Glass
Serve with Pickled Onion

Havana Cocktail—No. 2

1 dash Lemon Juice
¼ Dry Gin
¼ Swedish Punch
½ Apricot Brandy
Shake well
Strain into Cocktail Glass

Hawaii Cocktail

1 pony Dry Gin
1 pony Pineapple Juice
½ White of one Egg
1 dash Orange Bitters
Shake well
Strain into Cocktail Glass

Hawaiian Cocktail—No. 1

4 parts Dry Gin
2 parts Orange Juice
1 part Curacao
Shake well
Strain into Cocktail Glass

Hawaiian Cocktail—No. 2

⅔ jigger Applejack
⅓ jigger Pineapple Juice
1 dash Maraschino
1 dash Lemon Juice
1 spoon Sugar Syrup
Shake well
Strain into Cocktail Glass

Hearns Cocktail

1 dash Angostura
⅓ Whiskey
⅓ Italian Vermouth
⅓ Pernod's
Shake well
Strain into Cocktail Glass

Helen Florine Cocktail

½ Cognac
½ Green Crème de Menthe
1 pinch Red Pepper
Serve in Cocktail Glass

Hesitation Cocktail

1 dash Lemon Juice
¼ Whiskey
¾ Swedish Punch
Shake well
Strain into Cocktail Glass

Highland Cocktail

1 dash Orange Bitters
½ Scotch Whisky
½ Italian Vermouth
Shake well
Strain into Cocktail Glass

Hilliard Cocktail

1 dash Peychaud Bitters
⅓ Italian Vermouth
⅔ Dry Gin
Stir well
Strain into Cocktail Glass

Ho-Hum Cocktail

1 pony Bacardi
¼ jigger Lime Juice
1 spoon Honey
Shake well
Strain into Cocktail Glass

Holland Cocktail

⅓ Old Holland Gin
⅓ Orange Bitters
⅓ White Curacao
(A favorite at the Carlton Hotel,
    Amsterdam)

Holland Gin Cocktail

1 dash Angostura Bitters
1 jigger Holland Gin
Stir and serve in Cocktail Glass

Hollywood Cocktail

⅔ jigger Bacardi Rum
1 pony Dry Gin
1 spoon Grapefruit Juice
½ White of one Egg
Shake well
Strain into Cocktail Glass
Grate Nutmeg over top

Honeymoon Cocktail

Juice of ½ Lemon
3 dashes Curaco
½ Benedictine
½ Calvados
Shake well
Strain into Cocktail Glass

Honolulu Cocktail—No. 1

1 dash Angostura
1 dash Orange Juice
1 dash Pineapple Juice
1 dash Lemon Juice
1 jigger Dry Gin
A little Powdered Sugar
Shake well
Strain into Cocktail Glass

Honolulu Cocktail—No. 2

2 dashes Angostura
1 teaspoon Lime Juice
1 teaspoon Orange Juice
1 jigger Old Tom Gin
Shake well
Strain into Cocktail Glass
Twist Lemon Peel over top

Honolulu Cocktail—No. 3

⅓ Maraschino
⅓ Dry Gin
⅓ Benedictine
Shake well
Strain into Cocktail Glass

Hoop La Cocktail

¼ Lemon Juice
¼ Lillet
¼ Cointreau
¼ Brandy
Shake well
Strain into Cocktail Glass

Hoots Mon Cocktail

¼ Lillet
¼ Italian Vermouth
½ Scotch Whisky
Stir well
Strain into Cocktail Glass

Hop Toad Cocktail

Juice of ½ Lime
⅓ Jamaica Rum
⅓ Apricot Liqueur
Shake well
Strain into Cocktail Glass

Horse's Neck Cocktail

1 jigger Brandy
1 dash Angostura Bitters
Lemon Peel cut spiral
Place Peel in Highball Glass
    with end over rim
Add cracked ice
Add Liqueur
After shaking, fill with Ginger Ale

Hotel Bristol Special Cocktail

⅛ Contreau
⅛ Peach Brandy
Shake well
Strain into Tall Tumbler
(A favorite at the Hotel Bristol
    Bar)

Howard Wile's Cocktail

(6 People)
2 jiggers Dry Gin
2 jiggers Sherry
2 jiggers Dubonnet
2 dashes Crème de Cassis
2 dashes Apricot Liqueur
Shake well
Strain into Cocktail Glass
Add Cherry and Orange Peel

Hundred Per Cent Cocktail

1/6 Orange Juice
1/6 Lemon Juice
2/3 Swedish Punch
Shake well
Strain into Cocktail Glass

Hurricane Cocktail

⅓ Whiskey
⅓ Dry Gin
⅓ Crème de Menthe
Juice of two Lemons
Shake well
Strain into Cocktail Glass

Ichbien Cocktail

Yolk of one Egg
1 Port Wine Glass of Milk
¼ jigger Orange Curacao
¾ jigger Brandy
Shake well
Strain into Medium Glass
Grate Nutmeg over top

Imperial Delight Cocktail

Use Claret Glass
1 lump ice
3 dashes Fernet Branca
3 dashes Curacao
1 pony Brandy
Fill with Champagne
Stir
Squeeze Lemon Peel over top

Inca Cocktail

1 dash Orgeat Syrup
1 dash Orange Bitters
¼ Dry Gin
¼ Dry Sherry
¼ Italian Vermouth
¼ French Vermouth
Shake well
Strain into Cocktail Glass

Iris Cocktail

¼ jigger Dry Gin
¼ jigger French Vermouth
¼ jigger Sherry
2 dashes Orange Bitters
2 dashes Orgeat
Shake well
Strain into Cocktail Glass

Irish Cocktail

⅔ Green Crème de Menthe
⅓ French Vermouth
1 dash Orange Bitters
Shake well
Strain into Cocktail Glass

Irresistible Cocktail

1 pony Rum
1 spoon Lemon Juice
¼ jigger Italian Vermouth
1 spoon Benedictine
Shake well
Strain into Cocktail Glass

Jack Rose Cocktail

Juice of one Lime
⅓ Grenadine
⅔ Applejack Brandy
Shake well
Strain into Cocktail Glass

Jackson Cocktail

2 dashes Orange Bitters
½ Orange Gin
½ Dubonnet
Stir well
Strain into Cocktail Glass

114

Jersey Cocktail

½ Chartreuse
½ Cognac Brandy
Serve in Pony Glass

Joburg Cocktail

4 dashes Orange Bitters
½ Dubonnet
½ Bacardi Rum
Squeeze Lemon Peel on top
After shaking well

Jockey Cocktail

⅓ jigger Sloe Gin
½ jigger Italian Vermouth
1 dash Peychaud's Bitters
1 dash Cherry Cordial
Stir well
Strain into Cocktail Glass

Jockey Club Cocktail

1 dash Orange Bitters
1 dash Angostura Bitters
2 dashes Crème de Noyau
4 dashes Lemon Juice
1 jigger Dry Gin
Shake well
Strain into Cocktail Glass

John Cocktail

⅓ jigger Sloe Gin
1 dash Cherry Cordial
⅓ jigger Italian Vermouth
1 dash Peychaud's Bitters
Shake well
Strain into Cocktail Glass

John Collins Cocktail

Juice of ½ Lemon
(Collins Glass)
½ spoon Sugar
1 jigger Holland Gin
Shake and strain
Fill with Soda

John Holts Cocktail

2 parts Irish Whiskey
4 parts Italian Vermouth
2 parts Lemon Juice
1 part Kummel
1 dash Angostura
Shake well
Strain into Cocktail Glass

Johnnie Mack Cocktail

3 dashes Pernod's
⅓ Orange Curacao
⅔ Sloe Gin
Shake well
Strain into Cocktail Glass

Joker Cocktail

Use Sherry Glass
¼ Anisette
¼ Crème de Violette
¼ Benedictine
¼ Sweet Cream
Keep colors separate

Judgette Cocktail

⅓ Peach Brandy
⅓ Dry Gin
⅓ French Vermouth
1 dash Lime Juice
Shake well
Strain into Cocktail Glass

Jupiter Cocktail

1 teaspoon Orange Juice
1 teaspoon Parfait Amour
⅓ jigger French Vermouth
⅔ Dry Gin
Shake well
Strain into Cocktail Glass

Juschu Cocktail

1 jigger Tequila
2 teaspoons Strained Honey
1 teaspoon Lime Juice
1 dash Angostura Bitters
Shake well
Strain into Cocktail Glass

K.O. Cocktail

1 dash Apricot Liqueur
1 dash Lemon Juice
¼ Kirschwasser
¾ Dry Gin
Shake well
Strain into Cocktail Glass

Kicker Cocktail

⅓ Calvados
⅔ Cuban Rum
2 dashes Italian Vermouth
Shake well
Strain into Cocktail Glass

Kingston Cocktail

(6 People)
3 glasses Jamaica Rum
1½ glasses Kummel
1½ glasses Orange Juice
2 dashes Pimento Dram
Shake
Serve in Cocktail Glass

Kiss from Heaven Cocktail

⅓ Drambuie
⅓ French Vermouth
⅓ Cognac
Stir
Strain into Cocktail Glass

Knickerbine Cocktail

⅓ Crème de Rose
1 small Egg Yolk
⅓ Benedictine
⅓ Kummel
3 dashes Orange bitters

Knickerbocker Cocktail

1 teaspoon Raspberry Syrup
1 teaspoon Lemon Juice
1 teaspoon Orange Juice
1 piece Pineapple
⅔ jigger Rum
2 dashes Curacao
Shake well
Strain into Cocktail Glass

Knock Down Cocktail

1 teaspoon White Crème de Menthe
⅓ jigger Pernod's
⅓ jigger Dry Gin
⅓ jigger French Vermouth
Shake well
Strain into Cocktail Glass

Kummel Cocktail

1 pony Kummel
1 pony Dry Gin
2 dashes French Vermouth
Shake well
Strain into Cocktail Glass

Kungsholm Cocktail

1/6 French Vermouth
1/3 Liqueur d'Or
1/2 Rye Whiskey
Shake well
Strain into Cocktail Glass
Serve with Cherry

Ladies' Choice Cocktail

1 pony Kummel
1 pony Dry Gin
2 dashes French Vermouth
Shake well
Strain into Cocktail Glass

Lafitte Cocktail

1 teaspoon Dry Gin
1 teaspoon French Vermouth
1 teaspoon Pernod's
1 teaspoon White Crème de
   Menthe
Pour into glass of cracked ice
Shake—strain into Cocktail Glass

Lake Side Cocktail

¼ jigger Brandy
¼ jigger Crème de Menthe
¾ jigger Crème de Cocoa
¼ jigger Cointreau
Shake well
Strain into Cocktail Glass

Lalla Rookh Cocktail

1 pony Crème de Vanilla
½ jigger Brandy
½ jigger Jamaica Rum
½ spoon Sugar
1 tablespoon Cream
Shake well
Strain into Collins Glass

Lamp Cocktail

¼ Brandy
¼ Crème de Menthe
¼ Cointreau
¾ jigger Crème de Cocoa
Shake well
Strain into Cocktail Glass

LaZerwith Cocktail

⅓ Grape Juice
⅓ Swedish Punch
⅓ Dry Gin
Shake well
Strain into Cocktail Glass

Last Rose Cocktail

1 pony Port
1 spoon Sugar Syrup
¼ jigger Brandy
½ yolk of Egg
Shake well
Strain into Cocktail Glass
Grate Nutmeg over top

Last Thought Cocktail

1 pony Brandy
1 pony Champagne
Stir
Strain into Cocktail Glass

Lebow Cocktail

1 dash Lemon Juice
2/3 Dry Gin
1/6 Grand Marnier
1/6 Italian Vermouth
Shake well
Strain into Cocktail Glass
Squeeze Lemon Peel on top

Liberal Cocktail

1 pony Whiskey
1 pony Amer Picon
1 dash Sugar Syrup
Shake well
Strain into Cocktail Glass

Liberty Cocktail

1 dash Sugar Syrup
⅓ Cuban Rum
⅔ Applejack
Shake well
Strain into Cocktail Glass

Lillian Russell Cocktail

Add in order:
⅓ Crème de Rose
⅓ Crème de Violette
⅓ Sweet Cream
Serve in Pousse Cafe Glass

Lily Cocktail

I dash Lemon Juice
⅓ Dry Gin
⅓ Lillet
⅓ Crème de Noyau
Shake well
Strain into Cocktail Glass

Little Devil Cocktail

1/6 Lemon Juice
1/6 Cointreau
1/3 Cuban Rum
1/3 Dry Gin
Shake well
Strain into Cocktail Glass

Loensky Cocktail

⅔ Kummel
⅓ Scotch
Serve in Cocktail Glass

Louis Cocktail

⅔ jigger Dry Gin
⅓ jigger French Vermouth
1 dash Cointreau
1 dash Grand Marnier
Shake well
Strain into Cocktail Glass

Louis Special

⅓ Dry Gin
⅓ Benedictine
⅓ Green Chartreuse
Shake well
Strain into Cocktail Glass
(Courtesy of Louis Postenrieder,
   Head Barman, Hotel Bristol,
   Wien)

Lovers' Delight Cocktail

⅓ jigger Dry Gin
1 spoon Orange Ice
Shake well
Grate Nutmeg over top

Lune de Miel Cocktail

⅓ White Cocoa
⅓ Parfait Amour
Yolk of one Egg
⅓ Kummel
Pour separately into Sherry Glass

M. J. Cocktail

⅔ jigger Dry Gin
⅓ jigger Italian Vermouth
1 dash Crème de Cocoa
Shake well
Strain into Cocktail Glass

118

Ma Chérie Cocktail

⅔ Dry Gin
⅓ Cherry Liqueur
Shake well
Strain into Cocktail Glass

Madeleine Cocktail

⅓ Drambuie
⅓ Rum
Juice of ½ Lime
Juice of ½ Lemon
Shake well
Add 2 ice cubes
Serve in a Tall Glass
Filled with Seltzer

Mah Jongg Cocktail

1/6 Cointreau
1/6 Bacardi Rum
2/3 Dry Gin
Shake well
Strain into Cocktail Glass

Maiden Blush Cocktail

1 dash Lemon Juice
4 dashes Curacao
4 dashes Grenadine
1 jigger Dry Gin
Shake well
Strain into Cocktail Glass

Maiden's Prayer Cocktail— No. 1

⅛ Orange Juice
⅛ Lemon Juice
⅜ Cointreau
⅜ Dry Gin
Shake well
Strain into Cocktail Glass

Maiden's Prayer Cocktail— No. 2

1/3 Lillet
1/3 Dry Gin
1/6 Calvados Brandy
Shake well
Strain into Cocktail Glass

Mamie Taylor Cocktail

Juice of ½ Lime
1 jigger Scotch Whisky
Shake
Strain into Collins Glass
Fill with Fine Ginger Ale

Manhattan Cocktail—No. 1

1 dash Orange Bitters
½ Italian Vermouth
½ Rye Whiskey
Stir well
Serve with Cherry

Manhattan Cocktail—No. 2

2 dashes Curacao
1 pony Whiskey
1 jigger Vermouth
3 dashes Angostura Bitters
Stir well
Strain into Claret Glass
Serve with slice of Lemon

Manhattan Cocktail—No. 3

1 dash Angostura Bitters
⅔ Whiskey
⅓ Italian Vermouth
Stir well
Strain into Cocktail Glass
Serve with Cherry

Manhattan Cocktail—
(Sweet)

½ Italian Vermouth
½ Whiskey
Stir well
Strain into Cocktail Glass

Manhattan Cocktail—
(Dry)

¼ French Vermouth
¼ Italian Vermouth
½ Whiskey
Stir well
Strain into Cocktail Glass

Margot Belle Cocktail

¼ Dubonnet
¼ Orange Juice
½ Dry Gin
Stir well
Strain into Cocktail Glass

Marconi Wireless Cocktail

2 dashes Orange Bitters
⅓ Italian Vermouth
⅔ Applejack
Stir
Strain into Cocktail Glass

Marney Cocktail

⅓ Grand Marnier
⅔ Dry Gin
Stir well
Strain into Cocktail Glass

Martini Cocktail—(Dry)

⅔ Dry Gin
⅓ French Vermouth
Olive
Stir well
Strain into Cocktail Glass

Martini Cocktail—
(Medium)

¼ Italian Vermouth
¼ French Vermouth
⅓ Dry Gin
Olive
Stir well
Strain into Cocktail Glass

Martini Cocktail—(Sweet)

⅓ Italian Vermouth
⅔ Dry Gin
Olive
Stir well
Strain into Cocktail Glass

Martini Cocktail—(Special
Sweet)

1 dash Orange Bitters
½ Old Tom Gin
½ Italian Vermouth
Stir well
Strain into Cocktail Glass
Serve with Olive and slice of Lemon

Mary Ann Cocktail

⅓ Dubonnet
⅓ French Vermouth
⅓ Orange Juice
Shake well
Strain into Cocktail Glass

Marshall Cocktail

¼ Cherry Liqueur
¼ Dry Gin
½ Port Wine
Shake well
Strain into Cocktail Glass
Serve with Cherry

Maudi Cocktail

1 jigger Crème de Fine Champagne
1 dash Angostura
Shake well
Strain into Champagne Glass
Fill with Champagne and decorate

Maurice Cocktail

⅓ jigger Cognac
⅔ jigger Port Wine
Stir well
Strain into Cocktail Glass

Mayflower Cocktail—No. 1

½ New England Rum
½ Grapefruit Juice
½ teaspoon Sugar
Shake well
Strain into Cocktail Glass

Mayflower Cocktail—No. 2

¾ Dubonnet
¼ Applejack
Shake well
Strain into Cocktail Glass

McKinley's Delight Cocktail

1 dash Pernod's
2 dashes Cherry Liqueur
⅔ Whisky
⅓ Italian Vermouth
Shake well
Strain into Cocktail Glass

McMenomy Cocktail

2 dashes Grenadine
2 dashes Pernod's
Juice of ½ Lime
½ jigger Bacardi Rum
½ jigger Swedish Punch
Shake well
Strain into Cocktail Glass

Medford Cocktail

¼ French Vermouth
¼ Orange Gin
¼ Dry Gin
Shake well
Strain into Cocktail Glass

Merry Widow Cocktail

½ French Vermouth
½ Dubonnet
Stir well
Strain into Cocktail Glass

Metropole Cocktail

1 dash Peychaud Bitters
1 dash Orange Bitters
½ French Vermouth
½ Brandy
Stir well
Strain into Cocktail Glass
Serve with Cherry

Metropolitan Cocktail

⅓ Dubonnet
⅓ Cognac
⅓ White Crème de Menthe
Shake well
Strain into Cocktail Glass

Miami Cocktail

⅓ Cuban Rum
⅓ Cointreau
⅓ Lemon Juice
Shake well
Strain into Cocktail Glass

Mickie Cocktail

⅓ jigger Jamaica Rum
1 dash Grenadine
¼ jigger Curacao
¼ jigger Bourbon
Shake well
Strain into Collins Glass
Filled with ice
Dress with Fruit

Middleton Cocktail

½ Jamaica Rum
¼ Grenadine
¼ Holland Gin
White of 1 Egg
Juice of 1 Lemon
Shake well
Strain into Cocktail Glass

Mikado Cocktail

⅔ jigger Brandy
2 dashes Orgeat Syrup
2 dashes Crème de Noyau
2 dashes Curacao
2 dashes Angostura
Shake well
Strain into Cocktail Glass
Serve with Cherry

Millie Special Cocktail

1 jigger Jamaica Rum
1 pony Bourbon
1 pony Curacao
1 dash Grenadine
Serve in tumbler full of shaved ice
Decorate with Fruit

Millionaire Cocktail—No. 1

1 pony Whiskey
¼ jigger Grenadine
2 dashes Curacao
½ White of 1 Egg
Shake well
Strain into Cocktail Glass

Millionaire Cocktail—No. 2

1 dash Anisette
White of 1 Egg
⅓ Pernod's
⅔ Dry Gin
Shake well
Strain into Cocktail Glass

Millionaire Cocktail—No. 3

1 pony Whiskey
½ pony Pernod's
½ pony Grenadine
1 dash Curacao
½ White of 1 Egg
Shake well
Strain into Cocktail Glass

Millionaire Cocktail—No. 4

Juice of 1 Lime
1 dash Grenadine
⅓ Sloe Gin
⅓ Apricot Brandy
⅓ Jamaica Rum
Shake well
Strain into Cocktail Glass

Milwaukee Cocktail

⅞ Rye Whiskey
⅛ Apricot Brandy
Stir
Serve in Cocktail Glass
Add a Green Cherry

Mince Pie Cocktail

¾ pony Crème de Menthe
¼ pony Cognac
Serve in Pony Glass

Minneapolis Cocktail

1 pony Sloe Gin
¼ jigger Italian Vermouth
¼ jigger French Vermouth
1 dash Orange Bitters
Shake well
Strain into Cocktail Glass

Mississippi Mule Cocktail

2/3 Dry Gin
1/6 Lemon Juice
1/6 Crème de Cassis
Shake well
Strain into Cocktail Glass

Modern Cocktail—No. 1

1 dash Orange Bitters
2 dashes Jamaica Rum
1 dash Pernod's
2 dashes Lemon Juice
1 jigger Scotch Whisky
Shake well
Strain into Cocktail Glass

Modern Cocktail—No. 2

1 dash Orange Bitters
1 dash Pernod's
1 dash Grenadine
⅓ Scotch Whisky
⅔ Sloe Gin
Shake well
Strain into Cocktail Glass

Moll Cocktail

(6 people)
2 jiggers Dry Gin
2 jiggers Sloe Gin
2 jiggers French Vermouth
1 dash Orange Bitters
½ spoon Sugar
Shake well
Strain into Cocktail Glass

Monkey Cocktail

½ Cuban Rum
½ Pineapple Juice
1 dash Curacao
Shake well
Strain into Cocktail Glass

Monkey Gland Cocktail

3 dashes Pernod's
3 dashes Grenadine
⅓ Orange Juice
⅔ Dry Gin
Shake well
Strain into Cocktail Glass

Montana Cocktail

⅓ Brandy
⅓ French Vermouth
⅓ Port Wine
Stir well
Strain into Cocktail Glass

Monte Carlo Cocktail

¾ jigger Whiskey
¼ Benedictine
2 drops Angostura Bitters
Shake well with ice
Strain into Cocktail Glass

Moon Raker Cocktail

⅓ Brandy
⅓ Dubonnet
⅓ Peach Brandy
1 dash Pernod's
Shake well
Strain into Cocktail Glass

Moonshine Cocktail

1/2 Dry Gin
1/3 French Vermouth
1/6 Maraschino
1 dash Pernod's
Shake well
Strain into Cocktail Glass

Moose Cocktail

¾ jigger Whiskey
¼ Apricot Liqueur
1 dash Angostura Bitters
Stir well
Strain into Cocktail Glass
Add one piece Pineapple

Moulin Rouge Cocktail

3 dashes Grenadine
½ Apricot Liqueur
¼ Orange Gin
¼ Lemon Juice
Shake well
Strain into Cocktail Glass

Movito Cocktail

(5 oz. Glass)
Juice of ½ Lime
1 bar spoon Sugar
1 jigger Cuban Rum
Fill with water
Dress with Mint

Mufti Cocktail

1 pony Pernod's
¼ jigger Maraschino
¼ jigger Lemon Juice
Stir well
Strain into Cocktail Glass

Mule's Hind Leg Cocktail

1/5 Dry Gin
1/5 Benedictine
1/5 Calvados
1/5 Maple Syrup
1/5 Apricot Brandy
Shake well
Strain into Cocktail Glass

Napoleon Cocktail

1 dash Fernet Branca
1 dash Curacao
1 dash Dubonnet
1 jigger Dry Gin
Shake well
Strain into Cocktail Glass

Narragansett Cocktail

⅓ Italian Vermouth
⅔ Rye Whiskey
1 dash Anisette
Shake well
Strain into Cocktail Glass

National Cocktail

½ jigger Bacardi Rum
½ jigger Pineapple Juice
1 dash Apricot Liqueur
Squeeze of Lemon Peel
Shake well
Strain into Cocktail Glass

Natural Cocktail

1 pony Bacardi
¼ jigger Brandy
1 spoon Grenadine
1 spoon Orgeat
1 spoon Lemon Juice
Shake well
Strain into Cocktail Glass

Neapolitan Cocktail

¼ Grand Marnier
¼ Bacardi Rum
½ Cointreau
Shake well
Strain into Cocktail Glass

Night Cap Cocktail

⅓ Anisette
⅓ Curacao
⅓ Brandy
Yolk of 1 Egg
Shake well
Strain into Cocktail Glass

Nineteen Fourteen Cocktail

⅓ Orange Curacao
⅓ Sweet Cream
⅓ Dry Gin
Shake well
Strain into Cocktail Glass

Nude Eel Cocktail

¼ Dubonnet
¼ Chartreuse
¼ Cognac
¼ Dry Gin
1 dash French Vermouth
Shake well
Strain into Cocktail Glass

Number Three Cocktail

1 dash Orange Bitters
1 dash Anisette
¼ French Vermouth
¾ Dry Gin
Shake well
Strain into Cocktail Glass

Ocean Shore Cocktail

1 pony Sloe Gin
⅓ jigger Dry Gin
1 spoon Orgeat
5 drops Lemon Juice
½ White of 1 Egg
Shake well
Strain into Cocktail Glass

Odd McIntyre Cocktail

¼ jigger Lemon Juice
¼ Lillet
¼ jigger Cointreau
¼ jigger Brandy
Shake well
Strain into Cocktail Glass

Oh Henry! Cocktail

⅓ Benedictine
⅓ Whiskey
⅓ Ginger Ale
Stir well
Strain into Cocktail Glass

Ojen Cocktail

1 teaspoon Peychaud Bitters
1 jigger Ojen
Serve in Claret Glass with Seltzer

Old Etonian Cocktail

2 dashes Orange Bitters
2 dashes Crème de Noyau
½ jigger Dry Gin
½ jigger Lillet
Squeeze Orange Peel on top
Shake well
Strain into Cocktail Glass

Old Fashioned Cocktail

¼ lump of Sugar
2 spoons water
1 dash Angostura
Muddle Mixture in Old Fashion
   Glass
Add 1 jigger Whiskey
1 lump ice—stir
Dress with Fruits

Old Tom Cocktail

1 jigger Old Tom Gin
2 dashes Orange Bitters
1 dash Pernod's
½ spoon Sugar Syrup
Shake well
Strain into Cocktail Glass

Olsen Cocktail

½ Italian Vermouth
½ Russian Kummel
2 dashes Scotch Whisky
Shake well
Strain into Cocktail Glass

Olson Cocktail

⅔ jigger Whiskey
1 spoon Honey
⅓ jigger Cream
Shake well
Strain into Cocktail Glass
Grate Nutmeg over top

Olympic Cocktail

⅓ Orange Juice
⅓ Curacao
⅓ Brandy
Shake well
Strain into Cocktail Glass

One Hundred Percent Cocktail

1/6 Orange Juice
1/6 Lemon Juice
2/3 jigger Swedish Punch
2 dashes Grenadine
Shake well
Strain into Cocktail Glass

Opera Cocktail

1/6 Maraschino
1/6 Dubonnet
2/3 Dry Gin
Squeeze Orange Peel on top
Shake well
Strain into Cocktail Glass

Orange Blossom Cocktail

⅓ Orange Juice
⅓ Tom Gin
⅓ Italian Vermouth
Shake well
Strain into Cocktail Glass

Orgeat Cocktail

1½ tablespoons Orgeat Syrup
1½ jiggers Brandy
5 dashes Lemon Juice
Fill Glass with shaved ice
Shake well
Strain into Medium Glass
Dress with Fruits
Dash with Port Wine

126

Palisades Cocktail

1 pony Dry Gin
1 pony Cider
2 drops Angostura
Shake well
Strain into Cocktail Glass

Paradise Cocktail—No. 1

⅔ Bacardi
⅓ Apricot Liqueur
Shake well
Strain into Cocktail Glass

Paradise Cocktail—No. 2

⅓ Dry Gin
⅓ Apricot Brandy
⅓ Orange Juice
Shake well
Strain into Cocktail Glass

Pardo Bar Cocktail

1 jigger Cuban Rum
1 dash Amer Picon
1 dash Pernod's
Serve in Highball Glass
Fill with Seltzer

Parfait Amour Cocktail

½ Parfait Amour
½ Dry Gin
1 dash Maraschino
Shake well
Strain into Cocktail Glass

Parisian Cocktail

⅓ French Vermouth
⅓ Crème de Cassis
⅓ Dry Gin
Shake well
Strain into Cocktail Glass

Parisian Blond Cocktail

⅓ Sweet Cream
⅓ Curacao
⅓ Jamaica Rum
Shake well
Strain into Cocktail Glass

Passenger List Cocktail

¼ Brandy
¼ Dry Gin
¼ Parfait Amour
¼ Chartreuse
1 dash Pernod's
Shake well
Strain into Cocktail Glass

Passipe Cocktail

⅓ French Vermouth
⅔ House of Lords Gin
Juice of 1 Orange
Shake well
Strain into Cocktail Glass

Pauline Cocktail

(6 people)
3 jiggers Rum
3 jiggers Lemon Juice
1 dash Pernod's
Shake well
Strain into Cocktail Glass
Grate Nutmeg over top

Peach Cocktail

⅔ Peach Liqueur
⅓ French Vermouth
2 dashes Grenadine
Shake well
Strain into Cocktail Glass

Peach and Honey Cocktail

1 teaspoon Honey
1 jigger Peach Brandy
Stir well
Strain into Cocktail Glass

Peacock Cocktail

2 dashes Amer Picon Bitters
1 dash Pernod's
1 jigger Brandy
Shake well
Strain into Cocktail Glass

Peck Cocktail

½ Dry Gin
¼ Apricot Brandy
¼ French Vermouth
Shake well
Strain into Cocktail Glass

Peg O' My Heart Cocktail

½ jigger Lime Juice
½ jigger Bacardi Rum
1 dash Grenadine
Shake well
Strain into Cocktail Glass

Pegu Club Cocktail

1 dash Angostura Bitters
1 dash Orange Bitters
1 teaspoon Lime Juice
⅓ Curacao
⅔ Dry Gin
Shake well
Strain into Cocktail Glass

Philadelphia Scotchman Cocktail

1 jigger Applejack
1 jigger Port Wine
Juice of 1 Orange
Place in Tumbler
Fill with Ginger Ale

Philomel Cocktail

(6 people)
2½ jiggers Sherry
1 jigger St. Croix Rum
1½ jiggers Dubonnet
1½ jiggers Orange Juice
Shake well
Strain into Cocktail Glass

Phoebe Snow Cocktail

1 dash Pernod's
½ Brandy
½ Dubonnet
Shake well
Strain into Cocktail Glass

Phyllis Cocktail

½ Brandy
¼ Curacao
¼ Maraschino
½ teaspoon Lemon Juice
Shake well
Strain into Cocktail Glass

Picon Cocktail

½ Italian Vermouth
½ Amer Picon
Shake well
Strain into Cocktail Glass

Picon Pompier Cocktail

1 jigger Amer Picon
½ ounce Grenadine
Pour into Highball Glass
With cube of ice
Fill from siphon

Picon Whiskey Cocktail

1 pony Amer Picon
1 pony Whiskey
1 dash Sugar Syrup
Stir well
Strain into Cocktail Glass
Twist Lemon Peel over top

Pilgrim Cocktail

3/5 New England Rum
1/5 Lemon Juice
1/5 Cointreau
1/2 teaspoon Sugar
Shake well
Strain into Cocktail Glass

Ping Pong Cocktail

Juice of 1 Lemon
½ jigger Sloe Gin
½ jigger Parfait Amour
Shake well
Strain into Cocktail Glass

Pink Lady—No. 1

White of 1 Egg
1 tablespoon Grenadine
1 jigger Plymouth Gin
Shake well
Strain into Medium Glass

Pink Lady—No. 2

⅓ jigger Applejack
⅓ jigger Dry Gin
1 spoon Grenadine
1 spoon Lime Juice
Shake well
Strain into Cocktail Glass

Planters Punch

Juice of 1 Lime
1 jigger Jamaica Rum
Fill Tumbler with ice
Add Liqueur
Dress with Fruit
Fill with Seltzer

Platinum Blonde Cocktail

⅓ Sweet Cream
⅓ Curacao
⅓ Bacardi Rum
Shake well
Strain into Cocktail Glass

Plush Horse Cocktail

1 dash Angostura
⅓ Grand Marnier
⅔ Dry Gin
Shake well
Strain into Cocktail Glass

Poet's Dream Cocktail

⅓ Benedictine
⅓ French Vermouth
⅓ Dry Gin
Squeeze Lemon Peel on top
Shake well
Strain into Cocktail Glass

Pooh Bah Cocktail

⅓ Bacardi Rum
1 dash Apricot Brandy
⅓ Swedish Punch
⅓ Dry Gin
Shake well
Strain into Cocktail Glass

Poop Deck Pappy Cocktail

½ Blackberry Brandy
¼ Port Wine
¼ Cognac
Shake well
Strain into Cocktail Glass

Port Flip

¾ jigger Port
1 spoon Sugar Syrup
½ Yolk of Egg
Shake well
Strain into Cocktail Glass
Grate Nutmeg over top

Port Wine Nugus

½ tablespoon Powdered Sugar
1 jigger Port Wine
Fill Glass ⅓ with hot water
Stir
Grate Nutmeg over top

Pousse Café — (Paree)

⅓ Benedictine
⅓ Curacao
⅓ Kirschwasser
Pour separately into Liqueur Glass

Pousse Café—(American)

1/5 Maraschino
1/5 Curacao
1/5 Green Chartreuse
1/5 Anisette
1/5 Cognac
Keep colors separate
Serve in Liqueur Glass
Burn Brandy on top

Pousse Café—(St. Moritz)

1/7 Raspberry Syrup
1/7 Anisette
1/7 Parfait Amour
1/7 Crème de Violette
1/7 Yellow Chartreuse
1/7 Green Chartreuse
1/7 Cognac Brandy
Pour in order—keep separate
Serve in Sherry Glass

Pousse Café—(Rainbow)

Pour in order
1/6 Grenadine
1/6 Maraschino
1/6 Green Crème de Menthe
1/6 Yellow Chartreuse
1/6 Curacao
1/6 Brandy
Serve in Liqueur Glass

Pousse Café—(L'Amour)

⅓ Maraschino
⅓ Crème de Vanilla
⅓ Brandy
Pour separately into Liqueur Glass

President Cocktail

2 dashes Grenadine
Juice of ¼ Orange
1 jigger Cuban Rum
Shake well
Strain into Cocktail Glass

Prince of Wales Cocktail

⅔ Dry Gin
White of 1 Egg
⅓ Pineapple Juice
Shake well
Strain into Frosted Glass
(Made at the Hôtel Paris,
    Monte Carlo)

Princess Cocktail

¾ Apricot Liqueur
¼ Sweet Cream
Pour separately into Liqueur Glass

Princess Mary Cocktail

⅓ Dry Gin
⅓ Sweet Cream
⅓ Crème de Cocoa
Shake well
Strain into Cocktail Glass
Grate Nutmeg over top

Princeton Cocktail

¾ Dry Gin
¼ Port Wine
2 dashes Orange Bitters
Shake well
Strain into Cocktail Glass
Dash with Port

Prohibition Cocktail

½ Plymouth Gin
½ Lillet
2 dashes Orange Juice
1 dash Apricot Liqueur
Shake well
Strain into Cocktail Glass
Squeeze Lemon Peel on top

Prunelle Cocktail

¾ jigger Cognac
2 spoons Lime Juice
¼ jigger Prunelle Liqueur
Shake well
Strain into Cocktail Glass

Puritan Cocktail

1 pony Dry Gin
2 spoons Chartreuse
¼ jigger French Vermouth
2 dashes Orange Bitters
Shake well
Strain into Cocktail Glass

Quarter Deck Cocktail

1 teaspoon Lime Juice
⅓ Sherry
⅔ Rum
Shake well
Strain into Cocktail Glass

Queen Elizabeth Cocktail

½ French Vermouth
¼ Benedictine
¼ Lime Juice
Shake well
Strain into Cocktail Glass

Quelle Vie Cocktail

⅓ Kummel
⅔ Brandy
Stir well
Strain into Cocktail Glass

Quick Cocktail

⅓ Port
⅓ Grànd Marnier
1 dash Angostura Bitters
Shake well
Strain into Cocktail Glass

Rajah Cocktail

1 pony Brandy
1 pony Champagne
Stir with ice
Strain into Cocktail Glass

Razzberry Cocktail

⅓ jigger Applejack
⅓ Raspberry Syrup
⅓ yellow Chartreuse
Stir well
Strain into Cocktail Glass

Red Devil Cocktail

1 pony Brandy
1 pony Crème de Menthe
1 dash Red Pepper
Shake well
Strain into Cocktail Glass

Red Lion Cocktail

1/3 Dry Gin
1/3 Grand Marnier
1/6 Orange Juice
1/6 Lemon Juice
Moisten rim of Cocktail Glass
    with Lemon
Then dip in Powdered Sugar
Shake the Liquor
Strain into Cocktail Glass

Reform Cocktail

1 pony Sherry
1 pony French Vermouth
2 dashes Orange Bitters
Shake well
Strain into Cocktail Glass

Reno-Vator Cocktail

1 Egg
1 pony Benedictine
Shake well
Strain into Medium Glass
Fill with Cream

Rhine Wine and Seltzer

Fill Collins Glass
½ full with Wine
Fill with chilled Seltzer

Robert Burns Cocktail

1 dash Orange Bitters
1 dash Pernod's
¼ Italian Vermouth
¾ Scotch Whisky
Stir well
Strain into Cocktail Glass

Rob Roy Cocktail

⅔ jigger Scotch Whisky
⅓ French Vermouth
1 dash Angostura Bitters
Stir well
Strain into Cocktail Glass

Rolls Royce Cocktail

⅓ Cointreau
⅓ Cognac
⅓ Orange Juice
Shake well
Strain into Cocktail Glass
(Specially composed by Louis
Postenrieder, Head Barman,
Hotel Bristol, Wien)

Rory O'More Cocktail

1 dash Angostura
½ Irish Whiskey
½ Italian Vermouth
Shake well
Strain into Cocktail Glass

Rosa Cocktail—No. 1

¼ Grand Marnier
¾ Dry Gin
Stir well
Strain into Cocktail Glass

Rosa Cocktail—No. 2

¼ Cherry Brandy
¼ Kirschwasser
½ Dry Gin
Stir well
Strain into Cocktail Glass

Rosemary Cocktail

⅓ Whiskey
⅓ Grand Marnier
⅓ Lemon Juice
Shake well
Strain into Cocktail Glass

Rosette Cocktail

1 pony Dry Gin
¼ jigger Claret
¼ jigger Orange Juice
Shake well
Strain into Cocktail Glass

Roulette Cocktail

¼ Swedish Punch
¼ Rum
½ Calvados
Shake well
Strain into Cocktail Glass

Royal Romance Cocktail

⅓ Dry Gin
⅓ Grand Marnier
⅓ Orange Juice
Shake well
Strain into Cocktail Glass

Royal Smile Cocktail

¼ Dry Gin
¼ Applejack
¼ Grenadine
¼ Lemon Juice
Frappé well
Strain into Cocktail Glass

Ruby Cocktail

⅓ French Vermouth
⅔ Cherry Brandy
10 drops Acid Phosphate
1 dash Orange Bitters
2 dashes Maraschino
Shake well
Strain into Cocktail Glass

Rum Coffee Cocktail

1 jigger Jamaica Rum
⅔ cup Coffee
Stir and serve hot

Rum Collins Cocktail

Juice of 1 Lime
1 tablespoon Sugar
1 jigger Jamaica Rum
Stir
Add 2 pieces ice in Collins Glass
Add Liquor—fill with Seltzer
Stir again

Rum and Fruit Cocktail

½ jigger Jamaica Rum
½ jigger Orange Juice
1 teaspoon Kummel
1 teaspoon Benedictine
2 teaspoons Lemon Juice
Shake well
Strain into Cocktail Glass

Rum Sour Cocktail

Juice of ½ Lemon
1 jigger Rum
Shake well
Strain into Sour Glass
Dress with Fruit

Russian Cocktail—No. 1

⅓ Crème de Cocoa
⅓ Dry Gin
⅓ Vodka
Shake well
Strain into Cocktail Glass

Russian Cocktail—No. 2

1 jigger Cognac
1 dash Angostura
Use a Champagne Glass
Fill with Champagne

Russian Cocktail—No. 3

⅔ jigger Brandy
⅓ jigger Orange Juice
1 dash Orange Bitters
1 dash Pernod's
Shake well
Strain into Cocktail Glass

St. Germain Cocktail

Juice ½ Lemon
Juice ¼ Grapefruit
White of 1 Egg
1 pony Green Chartreuse
Shake well
Strain into Cocktail Glass

St. Moritz Cocktail

⅓ French Vermouth
⅓ Rye Whiskey
⅓ Gold Wasser
1 dash Orange Bitters
Shake well
Strain into Cocktail Glass

Sabbath Calm Cocktail

1 pony Brandy
1 pony Coffee
1 pony Port
1 whole Egg
½ spoon Sugar
Fill with ⅔ Cream
Shake well
Strain into Goblet
Grate Nutmeg over top

Sam Ward Cocktail

Cup a small Lemon
Fill with fine ice
Fill with Green Chartreuse

Sanctuary Cocktail

⅓ Cointreau
⅓ Amer Picon
⅓ Dubonnet
Shake well
Strain into Cocktail Glass

Sangaree (Gin) Cocktail

1 teaspoon Powdered Sugar
1 jigger Holland Gin
¼ glass shaved ice
Stir with spoon
Add 1 teaspoon Sherry
Serve in Cocktail Glass

Santa Cruz Daisy

Use Small Bar Glass
4 dashes Gomme Syrup
3 dashes Maraschino
Juice ½ Lemon
1 jigger Rum
Shake well
Strain into Cocktail Glass
Fill with Seltzer

Santiago Cocktail

½ Orange Juice
½ Cuban Rum
1 dash Grenadine
Shake well
Strain into Cocktail Glass

Santinas New Orleans Pousse Café Cocktail

¼ Brandy
¼ Maraschino
¼ Curacao
¼ Jamaica Rum
Pour into Liqueur Glass

Satan Cocktail

3 dashes Peychaud's Bitters
1 dash Pernod's
1 dash Italian Vermouth
1 jigger Bourbon
Stir well
Strain into Cocktail Glass

Satan's Whiskers Cocktail

2 parts Italian Vermouth
2 parts French Vermouth
2 parts Dry Gin
2 parts Orange Juice
1 part Grand Marnier
1 dash Orange Bitters
Shake well
Strain into Cocktail Glass

Savannah Cocktail

Juice of 1 Orange
1 jigger Dry Gin
White of 1 Egg
1 dash Crème de Cocoa
Shake well
Strain into Claret Glass

Self Starter Cocktail

⅛ Apricot Liqueur
⅜ Lillet
½ Dry Gin
2 dashes Anisette
Shake well
Strain into Cocktail Glass

Seven Fruits Cocktail

¾ jigger Whiskey
¼ jigger Seven Fruits
2 dashes Orange Bitters
1 dash Angostura
Shake well
Strain into Cocktail Glass

Seventh Heaven Cocktail

1 teaspoon Grapefruit Juice
¼ Maraschino
¾ Dry Gin
Shake well
Strain into Cocktail Glass

Sevilla Cocktail

½ teaspoon Sugar
1 Egg
½ jigger Port Wine
½ jigger Cuban Rum
Shake well
Strain into Cocktail Glass

Shaluta Cocktail

⅓ Dry Gin
⅓ Lemon Juice
⅓ Claret
2 spoons Sugar Syrup
Shake well
Strain into Cocktail Glass

Shamrock Cocktail

3 dashes Green Crème de Menthe
3 dashes Green Chartreuse
½ French Vermouth
½ Irish Whiskey
Shake well
Strain into Cocktail Glass

Shanghai Cocktail

2 dashes Grenadine
⅜ Lemon Juice
⅛ Anisette
½ Jamaica Rum
Shake well
Strain into Cocktail Glass

Sherry Cocktail — No. 1

⅓ Sherry
⅓ Lemon Juice
⅓ Dry Gin
Shake well
Strain into Cocktail Glass

Sherry Cocktail—No. 2

⅔ jigger Sherry
⅓ jigger Applejack
1 dash Angostura Bitters
1 spoon Orange Juice
½ spoon Sugar Syrup
Shake well
Strain into Cocktail Glass

Sherry and Bitters Cocktail

Use Sherry Glass
1 dash Angostura Bitters
1 spoon Orange Juice
1 jigger Sherry

Sherry and Egg Cocktail

¼ Claret Glass Sherry
1 Egg
Fill glass with Sherry

Sherry Flip Cocktail

1 Egg
½ spoon Sugar
1 jigger Sherry
Shake well
Strain into Sherry Glass
Grate Nutmeg over top

Side Car Cocktail

⅓ Lemon Juice
⅓ Cointreau
⅓ Brandy
Shake well—strain
Moisten rim of glass with Lemon
Dip into Powdered Sugar—serve

Silver Flash Cocktail

⅓ Benedictine
⅔ Sloe Gin
1 dash Orange Bitters
Shake well
Strain into Cocktail Glass

Silver Stallion Cocktail

½ Vanilla Ice Cream
½ Dry Gin
Juice of ½ Lemon
½ tablespoon Sugar
White of 1 Egg
Shake well
Strain into Collins Glass
Fill with Seltzer and stir

Silver Streak Cocktail

1 pony Dry Gin
1 pony Kummel
Shake well
Strain into Cocktail Glass

Singapore Sling—No. 1

Juice of ½ Lemon
1 pony Cherry Brandy
1 pony Benedictine
1 jigger Dry Gin
Shake well
Strain into Collins Glass
Fill with Seltzer
Dress with Fruit

Singapore Sling—No. 2

Juice ½ Lime
1 pony Grenadine
1 jigger Sloe Gin
Put Juice of Lime and
Shell into Collins Glass
Add 2 lumps of ice
Add Liquor
Fill from siphon and stir

Sir Knight Cocktail

⅓ Cognac
⅓ Cointreau
⅓ Chartreuse
2 drops Angostura Bitters
Shake well
Strain into Cocktail Glass
Twist Lemon Peel over top
Serve

Sit Down Striker Cocktail

⅓ Benedictine
⅓ Pernod's
⅓ Lemon Juice
Shake well
Strain into Cocktail Glass
Dash Cognac on top and serve

Six feet Under Cocktail

⅓ Bacardi Rum
⅓ Swedish Punch
⅓ Calvados
Shake well
Strain into Cocktail Glass
Squeeze Orange Peel on top

Sky Pilot Cocktail

⅓ Jamaica Rum
⅔ Applejack
2 dashes Grenadine
1 dash Lime Juice
Shake well
Strain into Cocktail Glass

Slam Cocktail

1/3 Cognac
1/3 Cointreau
1/6 Apricot Liqueur
1/6 Lime Juice
Shake well
Strain into Cocktail Glass

Sling—(Brandy)

½ lump Sugar
Dissolved in 2 spoons water
1 jigger Brandy
1 piece Lemon Peel
1 lump ice
Stir in Old Fashioned Glass

Sloe Gin Cocktail

1 dash Orange Bitters
⅔ Sloe Gin
⅓ Plymouth Gin
Shake well
Strain into Cocktail Glass

Snowball Cocktail

1/6 Crème de Violette
1/6 White Crème de Menthe
1/6 Anisette
1/6 Sweet Cream
⅓ Dry Gin
Shake well
Strain into Cocktail Glass

Sol Y Sombra Cocktail

1 pony Spanish Brandy
1 pony Dry Gin
Shake well
Strain into Cocktail Glass

Soother Cocktail

½ spoon Sugar
Juice of ½ Lemon
1 pony Brandy
1 pony Jamaica Rum
½ pony Curacao
1 spoon Apple Juice
Shake well
Strain into Cocktail Glass

Soul Kiss Cocktail

1/6 Orange Juice
1/6 Doubonnet
1/3 French Vermouth
1/3 Italian Vermouth
Shake well
Strain into Cocktail Glass

138

Southern Cocktail

Use Large Champagne Glass
½ Fresh Peach in Glass
Add fine Ice
Fill with Southern Comfort
Top with Cherry
Serve with Spoon

Southern Hospitality Cocktail

Use Champagne Glass
½ Southern Comfort
½ Champagne
Serve ice cold

Soviet Salute Cocktail

⅓ jigger Vodka
⅓ jigger Sherry
⅓ jigger French Vermouth
Shake well
Strain into Cocktail Glass

Spartan Cocktail

⅔ jigger Dry Gin
⅓ jigger Orange Juice
2 spoons Orgeat
Shake well
Strain into Cocktail Glass

Spion Kop Cocktail

½ French Vermouth
½ Amer Picon
Stir well
Strain into Cocktail Glass

Spring Feeling Cocktail

¼ Lemon Juice
¼ Green Chartreuse
½ Plymouth Gin
Shake well
Strain into Cocktail Glass

Star Cocktail

⅔ Applejack
⅓ Italian Vermouth
1 dash Grape Fruit Juice
Shake well
Strain into Cocktail Glass

Stars and Stripes Cocktail

⅓ Crème de Cassis
⅓ Maraschino
⅓ Green Chartreuse
Pour separately into Liqueur Glass

Stephens Cocktail

⅓ Sherry
⅓ French Vermouth
⅓ Benedictine
Shake well
Strain into Cocktail Glass

Stinger Cocktail—No. 1

¼ White Crème de Menthe
¾ Cognac Brandy
Stir—serve in Liqueur Glass

Stinger Cocktail—No. 2

1 pony Brandy
1 pony Crème de Menthe—White
Shake well
Strain into Cocktail Glass

Stinger Reserve

3 parts Rye Whiskey
1 part Pernod's
1 part Vermouth
½ Orange Juice
Shake well
Serve in Cocktail Glass
(Invented by Louis Postenrieder,
    Head Barman—Hotel Bristol,
    Wien)

Stinger Royal

⅔ Cognac
⅓ Peppermint Cordial
2 dashes Pernod's
Shake well
Strain into Cocktail Glass

Stone Fence Cocktail

2 lumps ice in Fizz Glass
1 jigger Whiskey
Fill glass with Cider

Straits Sling Cocktail

(6 people)
4 jiggers Dry Gin,
1 jigger Benedictine
1 jigger Cherry Brandy
Juice 2 Lemons
1 teaspoon Angostura
1 teaspoon Orange Bitters
Shake well
Strain into Collins Glass
Fill with Soda

Strawberry Cocktail

1 dash Orange Bitters
Juice 12 Strawberries
¾ Jigger Brandy
1 dash Maraschino
Shake well
Strain into Cocktail Glass
Add fresh Strawberry to top

Suburban Cocktail

1 dash Orange Bitters
1 dash Angostura Bitters
1/5 Port Wine
1/5 Jamaica Rum
3/5 Bourbon
Shake well
Strain into Cocktail Glass

Suisette Cocktail

1 Egg
Juice one Lemon
⅓ jigger Italian Vermouth
⅔ Brandy
2 dashes Pernod's
1 spoon Sugar
Frappé
Fill Collins Glass with Seltzer

Suissesse Cocktail

¾ jigger Pernod's
¼ pony Anisette
Shake well
Strain into Cocktail Glass
Fill with Charged Water

Sunrise Cocktail

¼ Grenadine
¼ Crème de Violette
¼ Yellow Chartreuse
¼ Cointreau
Pour separately into Cocktail Glass

Supreme Cocktail

1/3 Rum
1/3 Benedictine
1/6 Italian Vermouth
1/6 Lemon Juice
Shake well
Strain into Cocktail Glass

140

Sweet Dream Cocktail

⅓ jigger Dry Gin
⅓ Bacardi
⅓ Apricot Liqueur
2 dashes Pineapple Juice
Shake well
Strain into Cocktail Glass
Serve with Olive

Symphony of Moist Joy Cocktail

Claret Glass ¾ full shaved ice
¼ Crème de Rose
¼ Yellow Chartreuse
¼ Crème de Menthe
¼ Cognac Brandy
Berries on top

T.N.T. Cocktail

½ Bourbon
½ Pernod's
Shake well
Strain into Cocktail Glass

Tango Cocktail

1/5 French Vermouth
1/5 Italian Vermouth
1/5 Rum
1/5 Benedictine
1/5 Orange Juice
Shake well
Strain into Cocktail Glass

Tantalus Cocktail

⅓ Lemon Juice
⅓ Brandy
⅓ Forbidden Fruit
Shake well
Strain into Cocktail Glass

Tempter Cocktail

½ Port Wine
½ Apricot Brandy
Shake well
Strain into Cocktail Glass

Tennessee Cocktail

⅓ Whiskey
⅓ Maraschino
⅓ Lemon Juice
Shake well
Strain into Cocktail Glass

Tennis Girl Cocktail

¾ French Vermouth
¼ Scotch Whisky
1 dash Lime Juice
Shake well
Strain into Cocktail Glass

Three Fourths Cocktail

⅓ Yellow Chartreuse
⅓ Curacao
⅓ Brandy
Serve in Liqueur Glass

Three to One Cocktail

Juice ½ Lime
⅓ Apricot Brandy
⅔ Dry Gin
Shake well
Strain into Cocktail Glass

Third Rail Cocktail

⅓ French Vermouth
1 dash Orange Juice
⅓ Italian Vermouth
⅓ Dry Gin
Shake well
Strain into Cocktail Glass
Sugar edge of glass

Tipperary Cocktail

⅔ Sloe Gin
⅓ French Vermouth
1 dash Lemon Juice
Shake well
Strain into Cocktail Glass

Tom Collins

Juice ½ Lemon
½ spoon Sugar
1 jigger Old Tom Gin
Shake well
Strain into Collins Glass
Fill with plain Soda

Topper Cocktail

⅓ jigger Cognac
⅓ jigger Apricot Liqueur
⅓ Crème de Menthe
1 dash Pernod's
Shake well
Strain into Cocktail Glass

Trailer Cocktail

⅓ jigger Brandy
⅓ jigger Cointreau
⅓ jigger Lemon Juice
Shake well
Strain into Cocktail Glass

Trilby Cocktail

2 dashes Pernod's
2 dashes Orange Bitters
⅓ Parfait Amour
⅓ Scotch
⅓ Italian Vermouth
Shake well
Strain into Cocktail Glass

Tropical Cocktail

⅔ jigger Brandy
⅓ Crème de Vanilla
1 dash Peychaud's Bitters
Shake well
Strain into Cocktail Glass

Turret Cocktail

1/6 Grenadine
1/6 Swedish Punch
1/6 Calvados
1/6 Lemon Juice
1/3 Dry Gin
Shake well
Strain into Cocktail Glass

Twinkle Toes Cocktail

1/6 Orange Juice
1/6 Lemon Juice
1/3 Bacardi Rum
1/3 Swedish Punch
Shake well
Strain into Cocktail Glass

Vail Cocktail

¼ French Vermouth
¼ Benedictine
½ Rye Whiskey
Stir well
Strain into Cocktail Glass

Vermouth Cassis

1 jigger French Vermouth
1 pony Crème de Cassis
Use Medium Glass
Fill with Soda

Vermouth Cocktail—No. 1

⅔ jigger Italian Vermouth
1 dash Angostura
Stir well
Serve in Cocktail Glass
Add Pickled Onion

Vermouth Cocktail—No. 2

⅔ jigger French Vermouth
1 dash Pernod's
Shake well
Strain into Cocktail Glass

Vermouth and Curacao

1 jigger French Vermouth
1 pony Curacao
Use Medium Glass
Fill with Soda Water

Victory Cocktail

½ Grenadine
½ Pernod's
Shake well
Strain into Medium Glass
Fill with Soda Water

Virgin Cocktail

⅓ Forbidden Fruit
⅓ Crème de Menthe
⅓ Dry Gin
Shake well
Strain into Cocktail Glass

Volga Cocktail

⅔ jigger Dry Gin
1 spoon Lemon
2 spoons Prune Juice
Shake well
Strain into Cocktail Glass

Walford Cocktail

1 dash Angostura Bitters
⅓ Bourbon
⅓ Pernod's
⅓ Italian Vermouth
Shake well
Strain into Cocktail Glass

Wanda Cocktail

⅓ Kummel
⅔ Cognac
Serve in Liqueur Glass

Ward's Cocktail

½ Green Chartreuse
½ Cognac
Serve in Liqueur Glass

W. B. M. Cocktail

⅓ jigger Sloe Gin
⅓ jigger Brandy
⅓ jigger French Vermouth
Shake well
Strain into Cocktail Glass

Wedding Belle Cocktail

1/6 Orange Juice
1/6 Cherry Brandy
1/3 Dry Gin
1/3 Dubonnet
Shake well
Strain into Cocktail Glass

Which Way Cocktail

⅓ Pernod's
⅓ Anisette
⅓ Cognac
Shake well
Strain into Cocktail Glass

Whip Cocktail

¼ Brandy
¼ French Vermouth
¼ Curacao
¼ Pernod's
Shake well
Strain into Cocktail Glass

Whiskey Cocktail

1 jigger Whiskey
1 dash Angostura
1 dash Sugar Syrup
Stir well
Strain into Cocktail Glass
Twist Lemon Peel over
Add Cherry

Whiskey Blossom Cocktail

⅔ jigger Whiskey
⅓ jigger Italian Vermouth
1 dash Pineapple Juice
1 dash Lemon Juice
Stir well
Strain into Cocktail Glass

Whiskey Flip

1 Egg
½ spoon sugar
1 jigger Whiskey
Shake well
Strain into Cocktail Glass

White Cocktail

¾ Dry Gin
¼ Anisette
2 dashes Orange Bitters
Shake well
Strain into Cocktail Glass

White Cargo Cocktail

½ Vanilla Ice Cream
½ Dry Gin
Shake well—no ice
Serve in Cocktail Glass

White Lion Cocktail

2 teaspoons Powdered Sugar
    dissolved in water
Juice ½ Lemon
Put Lemon Rind in glass
2 teaspoons Raspberry Syrup
1 jigger Rum
½ pony Orange Curacao
Mix well in Medium Glass
Fill with shaved ice
Dress with Fruits

White Plush Cocktail

1 jigger Dry Gin
1 pony Maraschino
1 pint Milk
Shake well
Strain into Cocktail Glass

White Rose Cocktail

1 pony Gin
1 spoon Cream
¼ jigger Anisette
½ white of one Egg
Shake well
Strain into Cocktail Glass

Widow's Kiss Cocktail

¼ Parfait Amour
¼ Yellow Chartreuse
¼ Benedictine
Pour separately into Cocktail Glass
1 white of Egg beaten on top
Put slice of Strawberry on top

144

Wisconsin Cocktail

⅞ jigger Rye Whiskey
⅛ jigger Apricot Brandy
Shake well
Strain into Cocktail Glass
Green Cherry on top

Wonder Cocktail

1/3 Dry Gin
1/3 Claret
1/6 Sugar Syrup
1/6 Lemon Juice
Shake well
Strain into Cocktail Glass

Woxum Cocktail

½ pony Yellow Chartreuse
½ jigger Applejack
½ jigger Italian Vermouth
Shake well
Strain into Cocktail Glass

Yankee Doodle Cocktail

⅔ jigger Dry Gin
1 spoon Cream
1 spoon Crème de Violette
1 spoon Lemon Juice
1 spoon Sugar Syrup
Shake well
Strain into Cocktail Glass

Yankee Prince Cocktail

⅓ Apricot Liqueur
⅓ Pernod's
⅓ Yellow Chartreuse
Shake well
Strain into Cocktail Glass

Yellow Daisy Cocktail

(6 People)
2 jiggers Dry Gin
2 jiggers French Vermouth
1 jigger Grand Marnier
1 dash Pernod's
Shake well
Strain into Cocktail Glass

Yellow Glow Cocktail

⅓ Dry Gin
⅓ Yellow Chartreuse
⅓ Italian Vermouth
Shake well
Strain into Cocktail Glass
Add Stuffed Olive

Yellow Parrot Cocktail

⅓ Pernod's
⅓ Yellow Chartreuse
⅓ Apricot Brandy
Shake well
Strain into Cocktail Glass

Young Man's Cocktail

1 dash Boonekamp Bitters
2 dashes Curacao
¼ French Vermouth
¾ Cognac
Shake well
Strain into Cocktail Glass
Add Olive

Yvette Victoria Cocktail

¼ Crème Yvette
1 pony Pernod's
Pour Yvette into Cocktail Glass
Shake Pernod's with ice and pour
  over

Wally Cocktail—No. 1

1 jigger of Cointreau
1 jigger of Peppermint
2 jiggers Gin
Juice of ½ Lemon
Soda and Ice
Concocted by the Duke of Windsor
in celebration of his wedding

Wally Cocktail—No. 2

1 pony Brandy
4 dashes Benedictine D. U. M.
Lemon Juice to taste
Shake with ice and pour into
Champagne Goblet
Fill with Champagne

Zaive's New Orleans Cocktail

1 jigger Bourbon
1 dash Orange Bitters
1 dash Anisette Liqueur
1 dash Angostura Bitters
½ lump Sugar
2 dashes Pernod's
Shake well—strain into tall chilled
glass
Twist Lemon Peel on top

Zaza Cocktail—No. 1

1 pony Dubonnet
1 pony Dry Gin
Shake well
Strain into Cocktail Glass

Tropical Specialties

Bali Bali

¼ Barspoon Sugar
½ ounce Lime Juice
½ ounce Passion Fruit Syrup
1½ ounces Red Ronrico Rum
Shake all ingredients with enough
ice to chill. Pour into 10 ounce
glass, filled with cube ice and
decorate, using spray of fresh
mint, red and green cherry, and
colored straws.

Bingo—Bango

⅓ DuBouchett Sloe Gin
⅓ Q'Vana West Indies Rum
⅓ Pineapple Juice
Fill shaker with crushed ice. Shake
vigorously. Serve in Cocktail Glass
No. 9 or 10.

Daggar Palm

1 Barspoon Sugar
½ ounce Pineapple Juice
½ ounce Lime Juice
1 dash Curacao
1 spoon Pa-Pi-A Juice
1 dash of Port Wine
1½ ounces Red Ronrico Rum
Shake all with 5 ounce shaved ice
and serve in 10 ounce glass filled
with ice. Decorate with mint and
green cherry. Use colored straws.

Diablo

½ ounce Lime Juice
1½ ounce Ronrico White Rum
½ ounce Crème de Cassis
Shake well with 3 ounces of ice and
serve in 10 ounce glass ¼ full of
shaved ice and the rest with large
lump ice. Add Ginger Ale, round
of lime, red and green cherry.
Serve with colored straws.

Hurricane Punch

1 ounce Lime Juice
1 ounce Lemon Juice
2 ounces Passion Fruit Syrup
4 ounces Red Ronrico Rum
Shake well with 9 ounces shaved ice. Serve in 24 ounce special blue glass half filled with fine ice. Decorate with slice of orange, 2 cherries and colored straws.

Leon Mate Cocoanut Cooler

1 Barspoon Sugar
½ ounce Lime Juice
2 ounces Cocoanut Milk
1½ ounces Ronrico Rum, 151 Proof. Shake well with 3 ounces shaved ice till chilled. Then pour into cocoanut shell.Decorate with slice of orange, slice of pineapple, red or green cherries, colored straws, and serve.

Pago Pago Cocktail

½ ounce Lime Juice
⅓ ounce Green Chartreuse
1 dash Crème de Cocoa
1 stick Pineapple
1½ ounces Red Ronrico Rum
Muddle pineapple and shake by hand. Then strain into Cocktail Glass.

Pina Rico

White of one Egg
½ ounce Lemon Juice
½ ounce Passion Fruit
1½ ounces Red Ronrico Rum
Shake well with 3 ounces shaved ice to chill. Serve in fresh Pineapple with center taken out. Put top of pineapple back on and colored straws through hole bored just below the spines.

Polynesian Luau

½ ounce Lemon Juice
½ ounce Pineapple Juice
½ teaspoon Passion Fruit
½ ounce Crème de Prunelle
Dash of Ronrico 151 Proof Rum
1½ ounces Ronrico White Label Rum. Shake well with 3 ounces shaved ice.
Serve in Cocktail Glass.

Pontalba Punch

¾ ounce Orange Juice
1 dash Apricot Brandy
1½ ounce Ronrico White Label Rum
Shake well with 3 ounces fine ice and pour into 8 ounce glass filled with shaved ice. Serve with colored straws.

Port O'San Juan

½ ounce Pineapple Syrup
¼ ounce Curacao
1½ ounces Red Ronrico Rum
Shake well with 3 ounces shaved ice. Pour into 10 ounce glass with 3 cubes of ice. Add Club Soda, Float of Port Wine. Decorate with slice of orange and a red cherry. Serve with colored straws.

Rico Royal

1 teaspoon Sugar
½ ounce Lime Juice,
4 ounces Fresh Pineapple Juice
3 ounces Red Ronrico Rum
5 ounces Shaved Ice
Mir very well and pour into Highball Glass ½ full shaved ice. Decorate with orange, red cherry, stick of pineapple and fresh mint.

Ron Ricoco

¼ teaspoon Sugar,
½ ounce Lime Juice
3 Pineapple Sticks
1½ ounces Ronrico White Label Rum. Shake well with 3 ounces shaved ice and pour into cocoanut shell with 3 ounces cracked ice. Place cocoanut top back on and place straws through edge.

Shark's Tooth

¼ ounce Lemon Juice
1 dash Passion Fruit
⅓ ounce French Vermouth
⅓ ounce Sloe Gin
1 dash Angostura Bitters
1½ ounce Ronrico Gold Label
Stir with ice, strain into Cocktail Glass. Decorate with red cherry and twist of orange peel. Do not drop the orange peel.

Ronrico Loving Cup

1½ ounces Passion Fruit
2 ounces French Vermouth
4 ounces Ronrico White Label Rum
Shake well with 6 ounces shaved ice.
Place 36 ounces fine ice in special loving cup. Pour and decorate with half peach, red and green cherries, and 4 colored straws. Add 4 ounces Champagne and serve.

Sea Breeze Cooler

Use an 8 or 10 ounce glass
Fill with finely cracked ice
Over this pour 1 jigger DuBouchett Green Crème de Menthe
Fill balance of glass with more ice
Top with Seltzer. Stir gently to mix well. Garnish with red cherry and sprig of mint, which has been sprinkled with powdered sugar. Serve with two straws.

South Sea Dipper

1 barspoon Sugar
½ ounce Lime Juice
½ ounce Pineapple Juice
¼ ounce Passion Fruit
1 dash port Wine
1½ ounce Red Ronrico Rum
Shake well with ice to chill. Serve in 10 ounce glass half filled with shaved ice. Decorate with spray of mint, green cherry and colored straws.

Royal Hawaiian

1 spoon Brown Sugar
1 spoon Pa-Pi-A Syrup
1 ounce Lemon Juice
1 ounce Ronrico White Label Rum
½ ounce Dry Gin
1 whole Egg
Shake well and serve in 10 ounce glass filled with shaved ice.

Tahiti Club

½ ounce Lime Juice
½ ounce Pineapple Juice
½ ounce Lemon Juice
1 dash Crème de Prunelle
1 ounce Red Ronrico Rum
½ ounce Ronrico White Label
  Rum
Chill old fashioned glass and stir
  with cubed ice.

Tahitian Deep Purple

1 ounce Welch's Grape Juice
1 ounce Passion Fruit
½ ounce Lime Juice
1½ ounces Ronrico Gold Label
  Rum
Shake well with 5 ounces cracked
  ice and serve in 14 ounce Chimney Glass half filled with cracked
  ice. Use colored straws.

Tahitian Honey Bee

½ ounce Lime Juice
1 barspoon Honey
1½ ounces Red Ronrico Rum
Mix with 2 ounces Ronrico ice and
  serve in Cocktail Glass. Twist
  of lemon. Drop it.

Tahitian Rum Punch

½ ounce Lemon Juice
½ ounce Passion Fruit
½ teaspoon Sugar
1 dash Pernod's
2 ounces Ronrico White Label Rum
Shake well and serve in Highball
  Glass filled with shaved ice.
  Decorate with slice of orange
  and colored straws.

Zombie

1 barspoon Brown Sugar
½ ounce Lime Juice
1 ounce Passion Fruit
1 slice Pineapple
½ ounce Ronrico White Label, 86
  Proof
½ ounce Ronrico Gold Label, 86
  Proof
½ ounce Ronrico Red Label, 90
  Proof
½ ounce Ronrico Special, 151
  Proof
Shake well with shaved ice and
  serve in chimney glass filled with
  shaved ice. Decorate with round
  of lime, stick of pineapple, red
  cherries and colored straws.

Highballs

Admiral Highball

¾ jigger Whiskey
¾ jigger Tokay Wine
2 dashes Pineapple Juice
2 dashes Lemon Juice
Stir well
Strain into Highball Glass
Add Ice Cube
Fill with Seltzer

American Glory Highball

1 jigger Champagne
1 jigger Orange Juice
Stir in Highball Glass
Fill with Soda

American Picon Highball

1 jigger Amer Picon
1 pony Grenadine
Stir well in ice
Strain into Highball Glass
Fill with Seltzer

Applejack Highball

¾ jigger Applejack Brandy
1 spoon Lemon Juice
1 spoon Brandy
1 spoon Sugar Syrup
Shake well
Strain into Highball Glass
Fill with Seltzer

Bacardi Highball

1 jigger Bacardi Rum
Add one cube ice to Highball Glass
Fill with Seltzer—stir

Blue Heaven Highball

1 dash Pernod's
Juice of ½ Lime
1 jigger Scotch Whisky
2 cubes ice in Highball Glass
Fill with Ginger Ale and stir

Bon Soir Highball

1 pony Benedictine
1 pony Crème de Violette
Stir in Highball Glass
Fill with Ginger Ale and stir again

Brandy Buck Highball

1½ jiggers Brandy
Juice ½ Lemon
2 lumps ice in Highball Glass
Fill with Lime Rickey—stir

Brandy and Soda Highball

1½ jiggers Brandy
2 lumps ice in Highball Glass
Fill with Soda

Cassis Kirsch Highball

1 jigger Crème de Cassis
1 pony Kirschwasser
2 cubes ice in Highball Glass
Fill with Soda—stir well

Cider Nectar Highball

1 spoon Brandy
1 spoon Lemon Juice
1 spoon Sugar Syrup
Stir well in Highball Glass
Fill with Cider

Continental Highball

1 jigger Pernod's
1 spoon Sugar
Stir well
Strain into Highball Glass
Add ice cube and Seltzer to fill
Twist Lemon Peel over top

Durkee Highball

1 jigger St. Croix Rum
1 spoon Lemon Juice
1 dash Curacao
1 spoon Sugar
Stir well
Strain into Highball Glass
Add ice cube and Seltzer to fill

Egg Suissesse Highball

1 pony Pernod's
White of one Egg
1 spoon Orgeat Syrup
Shake well
Strain into Highball Glass
Add cube of ice and Seltzer to fill

Frozen Pernod's

1 pony Pernod's
1 spoon Sugar Syrup
Shake well
Strain into Highball Glass filled
    with cracked ice
Fill with Seltzer

Here's How

1 jigger Port
6 dashes Jamaica Ginger
1 jigger Brandy
Stir well
Strain into Highball Glass
Fill with Seltzer and ice
Grate Nutmeg over top

Horses Highball

2 jiggers Brandy
2 dashes Angostura Bitters
1 spoon Sugar Syrup
2 dashes Pernod's
1 spoon Lemon Juice
½ Egg (whole)
Grate Nutmeg over top
Shake well
Strain into Highball Glass
Add cracked ice and Seltzer to fill

Kirsch Fraisette Highball

1 jigger Kirschwasser
1 pony Strawberry Liqueur
Stir well with ice
Strain into Highball Glass
Add ice cube and Seltzer to fill

Kirsch Highball

1 jigger Grenadine
1 jigger Kirschwasser
Stir well
Strain into Highball Glass
Add ice cube and Seltzer to fill

Kiss Me Quick Highball

1 jigger Pernod's
2 dashes Angostura Bitters
4 dashes Curacao
Shake well
Strain into Highball Glass
Add ice cube and Selter to fill

Kitty Highball

1½ jiggers Claret
Stir with ice in Highball Glass
Fill with Ginger Ale

Magnolia Highball

1 jigger Brandy
2 spoons Curacao
1 Egg Yolk
2 spoons Sugar Syrup
Shake well
Strain into Highball Glass
Add ice
Fill with Champagne

New Yorker Highball

1 jigger Whiskey
1 pony Claret
1 spoon Lemon Juice
1 spoon Sugar Syrup
Stir well
Strain into Highball Glass
Add ice cube and Seltzer to fill

Picon Curacao Highball

1 jigger Amer Picon
1 pony Curacao
Stir well
Strain into Highball Glass
Add ice cube and Seltzer to fill

Picon Gomme Highball

1 jigger Amer Picon
1 pony Gomme Syrup
Stir well
Strain into Highball Glass
Add ice cube and Seltzer to fill

Port Light Highball

1½ jiggers Red Crème de Menthe
Stir with ice in Highball Glass
Serve with straws

Settler Highball

1 jigger Cognac
1 pony Crème de Cassis
Shake well
Strain into Highball Glass
Add ice cubes and Seltzer to fill

Shandy Gaff Highball

2 jiggers English Ale
Stir with ice in Highball Glass
Fill with Ginger Ale

Snow Ball Highball

1 jigger Whiskey
White of one Egg
1 spoon Sugar Syrup
Shake well
Strain into Highball Glass half full
  of ice
Decorate with Fruit in season

Starboard Light Highball

1 jigger Crème de Menthe
1 spoon Lemon Juice
Shake well
Strain into Highball Glass
Add ice and fill with Seltzer

Stone Fence Highball

1 jigger Whiskey
1 jigger Apple Cider
Shake well
Strain into Highball Glass

Vera Highball

¾ jigger Pernod's
1 spoon Sugar Syrup
Stir in Highball Glass with ice
Fill with ice water and stir again

Juleps

Brandy Julep

4 sprigs Mint in Mixing Glass
½ spoon Sugar
1 pony Brandy
1 dash Curacao
1 pony Water (then muddle well)
Fill Goblet ⅔ with fine ice
Add mixture—dress with Fruit
Decorate with Mint

Champagne Julep

1 lump Sugar in Goblet
3 sprigs Mint
2 lumps ice
Fill with Champagne
Stir gently

Georgia Mint Julep

¾ jigger Brandy
¾ jigger Peach Brandy
1 teaspoon Powdered Sugar
12 sprigs Fresh Mint
Place Mint in Tall Glass
Add Sugar dissolved in water
Stir well—serve cold

Gin Julep

2 jiggers Dry Gin
1 spoon Lemon Juice
4 sprigs Mint
1 spoon Sugar Syrup
Bruise Mint with Syrup and 1
    jigger water
Fill Tall Highball Glass with ice
Strain mixture into it
Add Gin—stir gently
Decorate with Mint

Jamaica Julep

Mash 6 sprigs Mint with Sugar and
    water
Strain into Bar Glass ½ full ice
Add 1 jigger Jamaica Rum
Shake—strain into Tumbler filled
    with shaved ice—add 3 sprigs
    Fresh Mint dipped into
    Powdered Sugar
Decorate with berries and other
    Fresh Fruits

Mint Julep—No. 1

Use Mixing Glass
Add 3 sprigs Fresh Mint
½ spoon Sugar
1 pony water
Then muddle well
Add 1 jigger Bourbon—stir well
Pour into tumbler ⅔ full ice
Fruit well—decorate with Mint
Dash with Jamaica Rum and a
    sprinkle of Powdered Sugar

Mint Julep—No. 2

1 jigger Brandy (or Whiskey)
4 sprigs Fresh Mint
1 pony Peach Brandy
1 spoon Sugar Syrup
Bruise Mint
Stir all in Highball Glass
Fill with ice and Seltzer
Decorate with Mint and Fruit

Pineapple Julep

Large Glass Jug ¼ crushed ice
Add Juice 2 Oranges
1 jigger Rasberry Vinegar
1 jigger Maraschino
1½ jiggers Dry Gin
1/5 Sparkling Moselle
1 whole crushed Pineapple
Stir well
Dress with Fruits and Mint

Prepared Cocktails For Bottling

Bourbon Cocktail

5 gallons Bourbon
2 gallons Pure Water
1 quart Gomme Syrup
2 ounces tincture of Orange Peel
1 ounce tincture of Lemon Peel

1 ounce tincture of Gentian
½ ounce tincture of Cardamons
Mix these ingredients thoroughly.
    Color with equal portion of Sol-
    ferino and Caramel to give the
    desired color. Then bottle and
    cork securely for future use.

Brandy Cocktail

5 gallons Strong Brandy
2 gallons Pure Water
1 quart Angostura Bitters
1 quart Gomme Syrup
1 quart Orange Curacao
Mix thoroughly
Strain through Canton Flannel
Bottle and cork tightly

Brandy Cocktail

5 gallons Strong Brandy
2 gallons Pure Water
1 quart Gomme Syrup
¼ pint Essence of Cognac
1 ounce tincture of Gentian
1 ounce tincture of Cloves
2 ounces tincture of Orange Peel
¼ ounce tincture of Cardamons
½ ounce tincture of Licorice Root
Mix the essence and the tinctures with a portion of the spirits; add the remainder of the ingredients. Color with equal parts of Solferino and Caramel to give the desired color. Then bottle and cork securely for future use.

Gin Cocktail

5 gallons Dry Gin
2 gallons Pure Water
1 quart Gomme Syrup
2 ounces tincture of Orange Peel
7 ounces tincture of Gentian
½ ounce tincture of Cardamons
½ ounce tincture of Lemon Peel
Mix well together
Give the desired color with Solferino and Caramel in equal proportions. Then bottle and cork well.

Gin Cocktail

1 quart Dry Gin
1 pint Orange Juice
4 jiggers Grenadine
1 pint Italian Vermouth
2 jiggers Lemon Juice
Stir well
Bottle for future use when desired for service
Shake well in ice and serve in Cocktail Glasses with Cherry and Orange Peel

Rum Cocktail

1 pint Bicardi Rum
1 pint Cointreau
1 pint Pineapple Liqueur (Crème de Ananas)
1 pint Lemon Juice
Stir well
Bottle for future use when desired for service
Shake well in ice and serve in frosted Glasses

Whiskey Cocktail

1 quart Whiskey
1 pony Orange Curacao
1 spoon Angostura Bitters
1 jigger Sugar Syrup
Stir well
Bottle for future use when desired for service
Shake with ice

Hot Drinks

Alhambra Royal

1 pony Cognac
1 cup Hot Chocolate
1 slice Lemon
Stir Cognac into Hot Chocolate
Add Lemon and serve

Apple Brandy

1 jigger Applejack
1 spoon Sugar Syrup
Stir with Hot Water in Highball
    Glass
Grate Nutmeg on top

Arrack Punch

Use large Bar Glass
1 teaspoon Powdered Sugar
2 dashes Lemon Juice
¾ jigger Arrack
Fill with Hot Water
Stir well
Grate Nutmeg on top and serve

Bacardi Grog

1 jigger Bacardi Rum
1 spoon Sugar Syrup
1 pony Hot Tea
Stir well in Punch Cup
Fill with Hot Water
Grate Nutmeg over
Serve with spoon

Black Stripe

Use small Bar Glass
1 jigger Jamaica Rum
1 teaspoon Molasses
Add Hot Water
Grate Nutmeg over top

Brandy Toddy

1 teaspoon Sugar
Dissolve in Hot water
1 jigger Brandy
Fill ⅔ with Hot Water
Grate Nutmeg over

Buttered Rum

(Highball Glass)
1 jigger Demerara Rum 150 proof
Spice to Taste
1 teaspoon Butter
Stir Rum and Sugar with Hot
    Water
Stir in Butter and Spice
Serve with spoon

Café Royal

2 spoons Yellow Chartreuse
1 cube Sugar
1 cup Hot Coffee
Place Sugar on spoon
Pour Chartreuse over
Until Sugar is dissolved
Add to Coffee and stir

Egg Nog

(Highball Glass)
1 jigger Brandy
2 spoons Sugar
2 jiggers Hot Milk
1 spoon Rum
1 Egg (whole)
Beat Egg to froth
Stir in Sugar, Brandy and Milk
Add Rum on top
Grate Nutmeg over top

French Egg Nog—
(Lait de Poule)

1 jigger Brandy
2 dashes Rum
2 spoons Sugar Syrup
Yolks of two Eggs
2 jiggers Hot Milk
Beat Egg with Sugar Syrup
And a little Hot Milk
Then add Brandy, Milk and Rum

Milk Toddy

1½ jiggers Rum (Brandy or
  Whiskey)
1½ jiggers Milk
Stir Liquor with Hot Milk in
  Highball Glass
Grate Nutmeg over top and serve

Gluh Wein

3 jiggers Claret
2 spoons Sugar Syrup
1 slice Lemon
Small piece Cinnamon
Bring to boil in saucepan
Pour into Highball Glass

Rum Punch

1 pint Jamaica Rum
½ pint Brandy
½ jigger Kummel
½ jigger Benedictine
Peel of one Lemon
Peel of one Orange
1 sliced Orange
1 sliced Lemon
Sweeten to taste
Add boiling water to Spirits
Stir well

Grog

1 jigger Rum
1 spoon Lemon Juice
1 spoon Sugar Syrup
Stir well in Highball Glass
Fill with Hot Water
Twist Lemon Peel over top

Tom and Jerry

Beat 6 Eggs well
Add Powdered Sugar till very thick
Stir thoroughly
Pour 1 teaspoon of Batter into mug
Add ½ jigger Brandy and ½ jigger
  Jamaica Rum
Fill with Hot Milk or Water
Grate Nutmeg over top

Key West

1 jigger Rum
1 spoon Sugar Syrup
½ spoon All Spice
Butter size of pea
Stir in Highball Glass with Hot
  Water
Grate Nutmeg over top

Punches

Ambrosial Nectar

(10 People)
2 quarts Burgundy
2 cans Sliced Pineapple
12 Sliced Oranges
1 Grated Cocoanut
Use Glass Mold
Build Fruit in layers
Sprinkling Cocoanut between each
Pour Brandy over and freeze
Turn out and serve in Sherbets

Archbishop Punch

1 jigger Port Wine
1 jigger Water
1 dash Rum
1 spoon Lemon Juice
1 spoon Sugar Syrup
Stir well with ice
Strain into Highball Glass
Add ice cube—decorate with Fruit
Fill with Seltzer and dash with
    Rum

Arrack Punch

Use Bar Glass
2 teaspoons Powdered Sugar
    Dissolve in a little water
2 dashes Lemon Juice
1 jigger Batavia Arrack
Fill tumbler ½ full of shaved ice
Shake well and strain into tumbler
Dress with Fruits in season

Bacardi Punch—No. 1

1 jigger Bacardi Rum
1 pony Curacao
1 pony Pineapple Juice
1 pony Grenadine
1 spoon Lemon Juice
Stir well in Highball Glass
Decorate with Fruit in season

Bacardi Punch—No. 2

¾ jigger Bacardi Rum
1 spoon Lemon Juice
1 spoon Cointreau
1 spoon Sugar Syrup
Shake well
Strain into Highball Glass
Fill with Seltzer
Decorate with Fruit

Baccio Punch

(8 People)
1 pint Champagne
1 pint Grapefruit Juice
1 pint Dry Gin
1 gill Anisette
Sugar to taste
1 pint Sparkling Water
Place in Punch Bowl and stir well
Surround Bowl with Ice and decor-
    ate with Fruit
Serve in Goblets with several fresh
    Grapes

Balaklava Nectar

(10 to 12 People)
Thinly peel rind of ½ Lemon
Shred fine and place into punch
  bowl
Add 4 tablespoons Powdered Sugar
Juice of one Lemon
1 gill Maraschino Liqueur
2 bottles Soda
2 fifths Claret
2 bottles Champagne
Stir well
Dress with Fruits

Bottled Velvet

1 quart Moselle or Rhine Wine
½ pint Sherry Wine
2 tablespoons Powdered Sugar
1 Lemon
1 sprig of Verbena
Peel the Lemon very thin and add
  only sufficient of the peel to produce the desired flavor. Add all
  of the other ingredients and stir
  well. Strain into a large Punch
  Bowl and decorate with Fruit.

Boland Punch

1 lump Sugar
2 wineglasses boiling water
1½ wineglasses Scotch Whisky
1 teaspoon Ginger Ale
Serve in Goblet

Brandy Punch

Juice ½ Lemon
½ spoon Sugar
1 pony Water
1 jigger Brandy
Shake well
Strain into Highball Glass
Dress with Fruit

Bombay Punch

(25 People)
Use large Punch Bowl
1 pound Loaf Sugar
2 bottles Apollinaris Water
1 Sliced Pineapple
6 Sliced Lemons
1 box Strawberries
Mix well and add:
4 fifths Champagne
1/5 Cognac Brandy
1/5 Pale Sherry
1/5 Madeira
1 gill Maraschino
Surround bowl with ice

Brandy Punch—No. 2

(Use Large Bar Glass)
2 teaspoonfuls Sugar in a little
  water
Juice of ½ Lemon
¼ wineglass Rum
1½ wineglass Brandy
1 piece Pineapple
2 slices Orange—shake well and
  strain
Fill Tumbler with shaved ice
Dress with Fruits and serve with
  straw

Brandy Champagne Punch

Use punch bowl with ice
1 jigger Brandy
1 pony Maraschino
1 pony Benedictine
1 Barspoon Sugar
1 fifth Champagne
1 pint Club Soda
Dress with Fruit
Stir well

Buda Punch

(10 People)
(Punch Bowl)
1/5 Champagne
1 quart Rhine Wine
1 jigger Orange Juice
1/2 jigger Orange Curacao
1/2 glass Bacardi
1 quart Soda
Garnish with Mint and Fruit

Brandy Shrub

1 quart Brandy
1 pint Sherry
¾ pound Sugar
Juice and Peel of 3 Lemons
Steep Lemon Juice and Peel in
    Brandy for 24 hours
Add Sherry and Sugar
Stir well
Strain through Jelly Bag
Bottle for use

Burgundy Punch

(12 People)
2 quarts Burgundy
1 pint Port Wine
½ pint Cherry Liqueur
Juice of 1 Lemon
Juice of 2 Oranges
¼ pound Powdered Sugar
2 quarts Sparkling Water
Serve in Punch Bowl surrounded
    with Ice
Decorate with Fresh Fruit

Bridge Punch

(12 People)
1 quart Claret
1 jigger Curacao
1 jigger Maraschino
3 jiggers Sherry
1 jigger Brandy
1 quart Seltzer
1 Sliced Lemon
4 jiggers Sugar Syrup
1 Sliced Orange
Place in Punch Bowl
Stir with ice
Decorate with Fruit

California Milk Punch

Juice of 4 Lemons
Rind of 2 Lemons
½ pound of White Sugar dissolved
    in hot water
1 Pineapple—sliced and pounded
6 Cloves
20 Coriander Seeds
Stick of Cinnamon
1 pint Brandy
1 pint Jamaica Rum
1 gill Batavia Arrack
1 cup strong Green Tea
1 quart boiling water
1 quart hot Milk—mix all well

Camargo Punch

1 pint Claret
1 pint Port Wine
Juice of 6 Oranges
½ pound Sugar
8 ounces Brandy or Rum
1 pint Sparkling Water
Serve in Punch Bowl surrounded with Ice
Decorate with fresh Strawberries or sliced Bananas

Canadian Punch

(10 to 15 People)
(Punch Bowl)
3 quarts Rye Whiskey
1 pint Jamaica Rum
7 Sliced Lemons
1 Sliced Pineapple
5 quarts Water
Sweeten to taste
Ice before serving

Cardinal Punch

1½ pounds Sugar
2 quarts Sparkling Water
2 quarts Claret
1 pint Brandy
1 pint Rum
1 pint Champagne
1 jigger Italian Vermouth
Stir well in Punch Bowl
Surround with Ice
Dress with Fresh Fruits

Century Club Punch

1 pint St. Croix Rum
1 pint Jamaica Rum
5 pints water
Stir well—dress with Fruits

Champagne Punch—Marco Special

(15 People)
8 ounces Strained Lemon Juice
16 ounces Deltour Reserve Cognac
8 ounces Simple Syrup
2 quarts Champagne Marco
1 quart Apollinaris

Champagne Punch — No. 1

Use Pitcher
1 pint Champagne
1 pint Sauternes
1 pint Apollinaris Water
1 Sliced Orange
2 lumps Sugar
Stir well
Ice before serving

Champagne Punch — No. 2

(15 People)
2 quarts Champagne
4 jiggers Rum
1 quart Green Tea
1 pint Brandy
1 can Crushed Pineapple
½ pound Sugar
1 Sliced Lemon
1 Sliced Orange
Stir all, except Champagne, in ice
Add Champagne
Decorate with Fruit

Champagne Punch — No. 3

½ pound Powdered Sugar
2 quarts Champagne
1 quart Sparkling Water
1 jigger Brandy
1 jigger Maraschino
1 jigger Curacao
Mix well in Punch Bowl
Surround bowl with ice
Dress with Fruit in Season

Charley Punch

Use Large Bar Glass
1 jigger Vermouth
1 jigger New England Rum
1 dash Orange Bitters
3 dashes Gum Syrup
Stir with shaved ice
Juice of ½ Lemon
Serve with slice of Fresh Peach

Chickadee Punch

(6 People)
1 quart Sloe Gin
1 jigger Jamaica Rum
1 pint Orange Juice
Juice of 3 Lemons
2 jiggers of Cherry Liqueur
2 tablespoons Sugar
1 quart Sparkling Water
Mix with Fruit Juices, Sugar and
    Syrups in a Punch Bowl
Place large block of Ice carefully in
    the center of the Bowl
Add the Liquor and stir well
Decorate with slices of Fresh Fruit

Cider Punch

½ pint Calvados or Applejack
½ pint Cognac Brandy
½ pint Orange Curacao
6 bottles Cider
2 large bottles Sparkling Water
Stir all well and strain into a large
    Punch Bowl
Add large block of Ice in the center
    and decorate with Fresh Fruit
    and sprigs of Mint

Claret Punch — No. 1

(15 People)
Juice of 6 Lemons
2 ponies Curacao
2 ponies Brandy
1 tablespoon Sugar
2 fifths Claret
Add ice and 2 siphons Soda

Claret Punch — No. 2

Juice of ½ Lemon
½ spoon Sugar
1 pony Water
1½ jiggers Claret
Ice well—pour into Goblet
Dress with Fruit

Claret Punch — No. 3

(Use Large Bar Glass)
3 teaspoonfuls Powdered Sugar
1 slice Lemon
2 slices Orange
Fill Bar Glass with shaved ice
Shake well with Claret
Dress with Fruit

Claret Punch — No. 4

10 to 12 pieces of Lump Sugar
1 bottle Sparkling Water
2 sliced Lemons
2 sliced Oranges
½ sliced Pineapple
2 jiggers Maraschino Liqueur
Mix well in Punch Bowl and place
    a large block of Ice in the center
    of the bowl. When ready to
    serve:
Add 4 bottles of Claret
1 bottle Champagne
Mix well and decorate with Fruit
    and Berries

Club Punch

2 fifths Champagne
1/5 Pale Sherry
1/5 Cognac
1/5 Sauternes
1 Sliced Pineapple
3 Sliced Lemons
Sweeten with Sugar to taste
Cool and serve

Coffee Punch

Place 4 pounds Sugar into a large
  dish
Pour 4 bottles Brandy and 2 bottles
  Jamaica Rum over the Sugar
Set this on fire—let Sugar dissolve
Drop this mixture into large kettle
  of Black Coffee
Stir well and serve in Goblets

Cold Ruby Punch

2 quarts Batavia Arrack
2 quarts Port Wine
5 pints Green Tea
2 pounds Loaf Sugar
Juice of 12 Lemons
1 Sliced Pineapple
Sweeten to taste
Ice before serving

Cosmopolitan Claret Punch

Use Large Bar Glass
½ goblet filled ice
1½ ponies Brandy
1 teaspoon Powdered Sugar
Fill with Claret
Shake well
Strain into goblet
Dress with Fruit

Curacao Punch

Juice ½ Lime
1 jigger Curacao
1 pony Cognac
Mix in Collins Glass with shaved
  ice
Dress with Fruits

Dragoon Punch

(12 People)
2 jiggers Brandy
1 quart Porter
½ pound Sugar
2 jiggers Sherry
1 quart Lager Beer
1 quart Champagne
2 Sliced Lemons
Stir all, except Champagne, in
  punch bowl with large cubes of
  ice
Add Champagne and stir again

Egg Milk Punch

1 Egg
2 teaspoons Powdered Sugar
1 jigger Brandy
1 pony Rum
½ glass shaved ice
Fill with Milk
Shake well and strain
Grate Nutmeg over top

Eldorado Punch

Use Large Bar Glass
2 teaspoons Powdered Sugar
1 pony Brandy
½ pony Jamaica Rum
½ pony Bourbon Whiskey
Shake well
Strain into Goblet
Dress with Fruits and ice

Empire City Punch

(50 People)
Use extra large Punch Bowl
Rub 4 Lemons and 2 Oranges with
Sugar until all of the color has
been absorbed by the Sugar
Mix well and add:
1/2 pound Sugar
1 Pineapple sliced fine
12 fine Sliced Oranges
1 box Strawberries
2/5 Apollinaris Water
1/2 gill Maraschino
1/2 gill Curacao
1/2 gill Benedictine
1 quart Jamaica Rum
1/5 Cognac Brandy
6 fifths Champagne
4 fifths Tokay Wine
2 fifths Madeira Wine
4 fifths Château Margaux Claret
Mix well with ladle
Strain through sieve into clean
bowl
Surround bowl with ice
Dress with Leaves of Mint, Fruit
and Berries

First Regiment Punch

1 pony Irish Whiskey
1 pony Scotch Whisky
1 teaspoon Powdered Sugar
3 dashes Lemon Juice
2 jiggers Hot Water
Stir well into tumbler

Fish House Punch

Juice ½ Lemon
½ spoon Sugar
½ jigger Brandy
½ jigger Jamaica Rum
Shake well—strain into tumbler
Dress with Fruits in season

Gin Punch

3 teaspoons Powdered White Sugar
1 pony Seltzer
1½ jiggers Holland Gin
4 dashes Lemon Juice
Shake well with fine ice
Dress with Fruit

Grandeur Punch

(25 People)
1½ pounds Sugar
6 Sliced Lemons
1 gill Anisette
1/5 Kummel
6 Sliced Oranges
1/5 Kirschwasser
1/3 gallon Water
6 fifths Brandy
1 gill Orange Curacao
Mix well in punch bowl surrounded
with ice
Dress with Mint and Fruits
Serve in Wine Glasses

Imperial Punch

2 jiggers Whiskey
1 spoon Curacao
2 spoons Sugar Syrup
2 spoons Lemon Juice
Stir well in goblet with cracked ice
Add 2 jiggers Champagne
Stir gently

Independence Nectar

(20 People)
1 quart Cognac
1 quart Champagne
2 pounds Sugar
3 quarts Claret
1 pint Green Tea
Juice of 24 Lemons
Stir all in Punch Bowl
When chilled, decorate
Serve in Punch Bowl

Hot Irish Punch

3 teaspoons Powdered Sugar
2 dashes Lemon Juice
1 wineglass Irish Whiskey
Fill with hot water—stir well
Serve with grate of Nutmeg over
   top

Kirschwasser Punch

1 teaspoon Powdered Sugar
3 dashes Lemon Juice
3 dashes Chartreuse
1 jigger Kirschwasser
Shake with shaved ice
Strain into Goblet

May Wine Punch

(Use a Large Punch Bowl)
Take 1 or 2 bunches of Woodruff
Cut in small pieces—place in Large
   Bar Glass
Fill with Old Cognac Brandy
Let stand for 3 hours
Cover bottom of Punch Bowl with
   Sugar
Pour over Sugar 5 bottles of Plain
   Soda
Cut 6 Oranges into slices
Slice ½ Pineapple
2 boxes Berries and Grapes
8 bottles Rhine Wine
1 bottle Champagne
Add Woodruff and Brandy, etc.,
   into Bowl
Stir well—surround Bowl with ice
Serve in Goblet

Medford Rum Punch

Fill glass with shaved ice
1 teaspoon Powdered Sugar
3 dashes Lemon Juice
1½ jiggers New England Rum
1 dash Jamaica Rum
Stir well and dress with Fruit

Milk Punch — No. 1

(Use Large Bar Glass)
1 teaspoon Powdered Sugar
1 jigger Brandy
1 jigger St. Croix Rum
½ jigger Jamaica Rum
Fill with fresh Milk—
Stir well and strain
Grate Nutmeg over top

Milk Punch — No. 2

1 glass Milk
½ teaspoon Powdered Sugar
1 jigger Rum or Whiskey
Shake well and strain into long
   tumbler
Grate Nutmeg on top

Mississippi Punch

1 pony Brandy
½ jigger Jamaica Rum
½ jigger Bourbon
1½ tablespoons Sugar
Mix well
Pour into tumbler filled with shaved
   ice
Dress with Fruit in season

Mulahat Punch

¾ jigger Brandy
2 spoons Pernod's
1 spoon Lemon Juice
1 spoon Sugar Syrup
Shake well
Strain into Highball Glass
Add cracked ice and Soda to fill

Old Navy Punch

1 fifth Demerara Rum 151 proof
1 pint Brandy
3 pints Champagne
⅔ pint Lemon Juice
1½ pounds Sugar
Juice of 3 Oranges
1 gill Peach Brandy
Stir well in Punch Bowl surrounded with ice
Dress with Fruits and Berries

Orchard Punch

(Use Large Bar Glass)
2 teaspoons Maple Syrup
3 dashes Lime Juice
½ pony Pineapple Syrup
Fill glass with shaved ice
1 jigger Brandy
Stir well--dress with Fruits
Dash of Port Wine on top

Orgeat Punch

(Use Large Bar Glass)
1½ teaspoon Orgeat Syrup
1½ jiggers Brandy
5 dashes Lemon Juice
Fill glass with shaved ice
Shake well—dress with Fruits
Dash Port Wine on top

Original Koenig's Punch

2 dashes Parfait Amour
1 Lime Peel in center of glass
1 jigger Rye Wiskey
3 sprigs Mint
Ice and fill with Seltzer

Oxford Punch

1 pint Cognac Brandy
1 pint Jamaica Rum
1 quart Orange Shrub
½ pint Sherry
1 bottle Capillaire
2 quarts boiling water
6 glasses of Calfs Foot Jelly
6 Lemons
4 Sweet Oranges
Dissolve sufficient Loaf Sugar in hot water
Rub rinds of 3 Lemons with Sugar
Cut peel off 2 Lemons and 2 Oranges thinly
Press out the juice of all the Oranges and the Lemons
Place all with the Jelly in a jug and stir well
Pour in the water and let it stand for 20 minutes
Strain through a fine sieve into a large bowl
Add Capillaire, Spirits, Shrub, and Wine
Stir well and serve hot

Pacific Punch

(20 People)
2 quarts Champagne
2 jiggers Curacao
1 pound Sugar
1 quart Cognac
1 quart Seltzer
Juice of 10 Lemons
Stir all, except Champagne, in Punch Bowl, with large cubes of ice
When chilled, add Champagne
Decorate and serve in Punch Cups

Parachute Punch

1 jigger Brandy
1 jigger Coffee
1 jigger Kirschwasser
½ white of 1 Egg
Shake well
Strain into Goblet
Add cracked ice
Fill with Seltzer

Peace Cup Punch

(12 People)
3 pints Champagne
3 jiggers Maraschino
3 jiggers Brandy
1 box Strawberries
1 pound Sugar
1 slice Pineapple
1½ quarts Seltzer
Crush Fruit with Sugar
Place in Punch Bowl with ice
Add Liquors and stir well
Add Seltzer and stir

Philadelphia Punch

(Use Large Bar Glass)
2 teaspoons Powdered Sugar
1 dash Lemon Juice
1 jigger Rum
1 pony Brandy
Stir well—dress with Fruit

Pineapple Punch

(25 People)
10 fifths Champagne
3 pints Jamaica Rum
3 pints Brandy
3 gills Curacao
Juice of 8 Lemons
6 Sliced Pineapples

Sweeten to taste with Powdered
Sugar
Mix in Punch Bowl surrounded
with ice
Dress with Mint and Berries

Ping Pong Punch

Use Pitcher
5 siphons of Soda
1 quart Whiskey
1 quart Brandy
Crushed Mint and Fruit
Stir well and serve

Plymouth Punch

¼ Lemon Peel
½ tablespoon Sugar
Muddle in glass
⅓ jigger Sloe Gin
⅔ jigger Rye Whiskey
Stir well
Strain into Champagne Glass
Add ½ Fresh Peach
2 dashes Rum and serve

Princeton Punch

¼ Lime Peel
½ tablespoon Sugar
Muddle in glass
⅓ jigger Sloe Gin
⅔ jigger French Vermouth
Stir well
Strain into Burgundy glass
Add dash of Bitters

Punch à la King

2 lbs. Loaf Sugar
3 dozen Lemons
1 pint Cognac
1 pint Jamaica Rum
Peel the Lemons and place them into a jar with the Sugar
Stir well for an hour to extract the oil. Add some boiling water and stir until the Sugar is dissolved.
Cut and squeeze the Lemons. Strain the juice and place the pits into another jar. Pour some boiling water on them to extract the mucilage from them. Pour ½ of the Lemon Juice into the Sugar Syrup, Strain the water from the pits and add it to the Syrup also. Then add more Sugar or Lemon Juice according to your taste.
Then add the above amount of spirits to every 3 qts. of Lemonade.
Stir well, place in bottles and keep in a cool place until ready for use.

Punch à la Marmora

1 pint Orgeat Syrup
⅓ pint Cognac
1 gill Maraschino Liqueur
1 gill Jamaica Rum
1 bottle Champagne
1 bottle Soda
3 ozs. Sugar Syrup
2 sliced Lemons
2 sliced Oranges
Several slices of Pineapple
Stir all well with ladle and place into Punch Bowl with large block of Ice in center
Decorate with fresh Fruit and serve

Punch à la Romaine

(Serves 10 to 15 People)
1 bottle Rum
1 bottle Wine
10 Lemons
2 Sweet Oranges
2 pounds of Powdered Sugar
10 Eggs
Dissolve Sugar with Lemons and Orange Juice
Add rind of 1 Orange
Strain through sieve into a bowl
Add the whites of the Eggs beaten to a froth
Place bowl on ice and stir well, adding the Rum and the Wine

Punch Brumonia

Juice of ½ Orange
½ spoon Sugar
1 pony water
1 jigger Rum
Shake well
Strain into goblet ⅔ full of ice
Dress with Fresh fruit

Punch Royal

1 pint Cognac
1 quart Sherry
2 jiggers Grenadine
1 jigger Lemon Juice
2 pounds Sugar
4 jiggers Apricot Brandy
1 pint Sauternes
3 jiggers Orange Juice
1 jigger Grape Fruit Juice
3 sprigs Mint
4/5 Ginger Ale
Crush Mint with Sugar in Punch Bowl
Add other ingredients with ice cubes
Stir well
Decorate with Fruit

Punch Universal

2 tablespoons Sugar
Juice of 2 Lemons
Juice of 1 Orange
1 pony Jamaica Rum
1 pony Brandy
1 bottle Club Soda
1 fifth Chablis
Ice and Fruit Well

Regent Punch

1 sliced Lemon
1 sliced Orange
1 can Pineapple and the juice
2 jiggers Rum
4 jiggers Bourbon
18 lumps Sugar
Mix well in a Punch Bowl and let
    stand 2 hours in cold place
Add pint of Tea and mix slowly
When ready to serve add a quart
    of Champagne

Rhine Wine Punch

(8 People)
2 quarts Rhine or Moselle Wine
2 jiggers Grape Brandy
1 jigger Maraschino Liqueur
2 tablespoons Sugar
6 ounces strong Tea
1 quart Sparkling Water
Mix well in Punch Bowl
Add large block of Ice
Dress with fresh Fruit

Roman Punch

Juice of ½ Lemon
1 spoon Sugar
1 pony Curacao
½ jigger Jamaica Rum
½ jigger Brandy
2 dashes Port Wine
Shake well—strain into tumbler
Fruit well—fill with Soda

Rosita Punch

(8 People)
7 jiggers Orange Juice
3 jiggers Lemon Juice
1 cup crushed Pineapple
1 cup Cherry Liqueur
1 cup Sugar Syrup
1 cup Green Tea
1 qt. Cuban Rum
1 jigger Jamaica Rum
1 quart Sparkling Water

Royal Punch

(Use a Large Mixing Bowl)
1 pint hot Green Tea
1 pint Cognac
½ pint Jamaica Rum
1 jigger Orange Curacao
1 jigger Arrack
Juice of 2 Limes
1 sliced Lemon
½ pound Sugar
Mix well with ladle and add whites
    of 4 Eggs
Serve very hot

Rum Punch

Juice of ½ Lemon
½ spoon Sugar
1 pony Water
1 jigger Rum
Shake well
Strain into Goblet ⅔ full of ice
Dress with Fruit

Rum Punch

(8 People)
1 quart Rum
1 quart Orange Juice
½ pound Sugar
Stir well
Strain through Jelly Bag
Bottle for use

168

Russian Claret Punch

1½ bottles Claret
3 jiggers Curacao
½ pint Sherry
3 jiggers Brandy
1 jigger Raspberry Syrup
1½ Oranges sliced
½ Lemon sliced
1 bottle Seltzer
1½ bottles Soda Water
Stir all together well and add some sprigs of Balm and Borage and a small piece of Cucumber Rind, sweeten with Sugar Syrup to taste and let it ferment for one hour. Strain into a large Punch Bowl and surround with Ice. When very cold serve in small glasses.

Sauternes Punch

3 teaspoons Powdered Sugar
1 slice Lemon
2 slices Orange
Fill Bar Glass with shaved ice
Fill with Sauternes
Shake well—dress with Fruit
Serve with straw

Scotch Punch

Melt 1 lump Sugar in cold water
Strain juice of two Lemons through fine hair strainer, and add to sugar and water
Add Jamaica Rum—1 part to five parts of Sherbet
Cut a Lime in half. Run each half over the rim of the glass, gently squeezing in some of the juice
The punch is then ready for serving

Second Regiment Punch

(Use Large Bar Glass)
2 teaspoons Powdered Sugar
3 dashes Lemon Juice
1 jigger Brandy
1 jigger Muscatel
Flavor with Raspberry Syrup
Fill Bar Glass with fine ice
Shake well—dress with Fruits
Dash of Jamaica Rum

Sherry Wine Punch

(Use Large Bar Glass)
Fill glass with shaved ice
2 jiggers Sherry
2 teaspoons Powdered Sugar
3 dashes Lemon Juice
Stir well—dress with Fruits
Dash with Claret

St. Charles Punch

(Use Large Bar Glass)
2 teaspoons Powdered Sugar
¼ juice of Lemon
1 jigger Port Wine
1 jigger Brandy
Fill with shaved ice
Shake well — dress with Fruit

St. Croix Rum Punch

2 teaspoons Powdered Sugar
3 dashes Lemon Juice
2 dashes Jamaica Rum
1 jigger St. Croix Rum
Fill with shaved ice
Dress with Fruit

Tea Punch

1½ jiggers Brandy
2 jiggers Hot Tea
1 spoon Sugar Syrup
2 spoons Rum
1 spoon Lemon Juice
Stir well in Highball Glass
Twist Lemon Peel over top

Tempter Punch

(For a party of 15)
¾ pound Loaf Sugar
Juice of 3 Oranges (strained)
Add juice to Sugar along with part
    of the Orange Rind
Add a quart of boiling water
11 ounces Batavia Arrack
1 bottle hot Claret
Stir well and let stand
Serve cold

Tip Top Punch

Use Large Bar Glass
½ jigger Brandy
1 spoon Powdered Sugar
2 slices Pineapple
2 slices Orange
2 dashes Lemon Juice
Stir in glass ¼ full ice
Fill with Champagne and stir again
Dress with Fruit

Tobies Punch

2 large Lemons
Several large lumps Sugar
Rub Sugar over Lemons until Sugar
    has absorbed all of the yellow
    part of the skins
Place these lumps of Sugar into a
    Bowl with the juice of the two
    Lemons. Add more Sugar to taste,
    up to ½ lb.
Muddle the Juice and the Sugar well
Mix this well with boiling water
Add 1 pint Brandy and 1 pint Rum

Toledo Punch

(Use Large Punch Bowl)
2½ pounds Loaf Sugar
6 bottles Plain Soda
Juice of 4 Lemons
1 quart Cognac
1 small bunch Wintergreen
4 sliced Oranges
1 sliced Pineapple
1 box Strawberries
1 box Grapes
Mix well and add:
6 fifths Champagne
1 fifth Brandy
4 fifths Claret
4 fifths Rhine Wine
1½ gallons Water
Stir again
Surround bowl with ice
Allow to ferment for two hours

Vanilla Punch

(Use Large Bar Glass)
2 teaspoons Powdered Sugar in a
   little water
3 dashes Lemon Juice
3 dashes Curacao
1 jigger Brandy
1 pony Vanilla Cordial
Fill with shaved ice—mix well
Dress with Fruit

Vaulter Punch

2 jiggers Whiskey
Stir Whiskey with fine ice
Add 2 pieces Lemon Peel
Strain into Goblet filled with
   cracked ice
Fill with Cider
Decorate with Fruit

Warzana Punch

1 quart Claret
1 quart Champagne
2 jiggers Cointreau
2 jiggers Jamaica Rum
2 jiggers Orange Juice
2 jiggers Lemon Juice
1 quart Sparkling Water
Place all in Punch Bowl and stir
   well. Add large piece of ice in
   center of bowl and decorate with
   Fruit

Whiskey Punch

Juice of ½ Lemon
½ spoon Sugar
1 pony Water
Fill glass ⅔ fine ice
Add mixture
1 jigger Whiskey
Stir well
Decorate with Fruit

Whiskey Punch (Hot)

Juice of ½ Lemon
3 teaspoons Powdered Sugar
1 jigger hot water
2 jiggers Scotch
Place all in Whiskey Glass
Add slice of Lemon
Grate Nutmeg over top

White Wine Punch

1 jigger White Wine
1 spoon Arrack Punch
1 spoon Sugar Syrup
Stir well
Strain into Highball Glass
Add one cube of ice
Fill with Seltzer
Decorate with Fruit

Yucatan Punch

(6 People)
1 pint Jamaica Rum
1 quart Dry Sherry
3 whipped White of Egg
Juice of 4 Lemons
Juice of 2 Oranges
6 ounces Sugar
1 pint Soda
Shake well and serve
Decorate with Fruit

Coolers

Apricot Cooler

Juice ½ Lemon
2 dashes Grenadine
1 pony Apricot Liqueur
Shake well
Strain into Highball Glass
Fill with Soda Water

Arrack Cooler

¾ jigger Arrack
1 dash Champagne
1 spoon Sugar Syrup
¼ jigger Rum
1 spoon Lemon Juice
Shake all, except Champagne, with
   ice — strain into goblet, add ice
   cube, Champagne and Seltzer

Boston Cooler

Juice ½ Lemon
¼ spoon Sugar
1 jigger New England Rum
Shake well
Strain into Highball Glass
Fill with Plain Soda

Brandy Cooler

1½ jiggers Brandy
Place twisted Lemon Peel in goblet,
Add Ginger Ale to fill
   add cracked ice and Brandy, stir
   well

Bulldog Cooler

1½ jiggers Dry Gin
1 spoon Sugar
1 spoon Lemon
Stir well with ice and strain into
   Highball Glass
Add ice cube and Ginger Ale

Harvard Cooler

Juice ½ Lemon
½ tablespoon Sugar
1 jigger Applejack
Shake well
Strain into Highball Glass
Fill with Plain Soda

Highland Cooler

1 teaspoon Powdered Sugar
Juice of ½ Lemon
2 dashes Angostura Bitters
1 jigger Scotch Whisky
1 lump ice
Use Long Tumbler
Fill with Ginger Ale

Klondike Cooler

Whole peel of one Orange
Juice of one Orange
1 jigger Whiskey
1 lump ice
Serve in Collins Glass
Fill with Ginger Ale

Lone Tree Cooler

Juice of ½ Lemon
Juice of one Orange
⅓ French Vermouth
⅔ Dry Gin
1 pony Grenadine
Shake well
Strain into Tumbler
Fill with Soda

Missouri Cooler

1 jigger Applejack
2 jiggers Milk
1 spoon Sugar Syrup
1 pony Crème de Cocoa
Shake well with ice
Strain into Goblet
Grate Nutmeg over top

Missouri Mule

1 Jigger 100 Proof Southern
    Comfort
Juice of ¼ Lime
Cracked Ice and fill with Ginger
    Beer

Moscow Mule

1 Jigger Smirnoff Vodka
½ Lime
2 Cubes of Ice
Fill Copper Mug with Cock 'n Bull
    Ginger Beer

Remsen Cooler

2 jiggers gin
1 spoon Sugar Syrup
6 pieces Lemon Peel
Bruise Peel with Syrup in Highball
    Glass
Add cracked ice, Gin and Soda to
    fill

Reviver Cooler

1 jigger Brandy
½ jigger Framboise Liqueur
2 jiggers Milk
Shake well with ice
Strain into Goblet
Add cracked ice and Soda to fill

Rocky Mountain Cooler

1 jigger Applejack Brandy
1 Egg
1 spoon Sugar Syrup
1 spoon Lemon Juice
Fill with Cider
Shake well with ice
Grate Nutmeg over top

Sauternes Cooler

3 jiggers Sauternes
2 teaspoons Lemon Juice
1 spoon Sugar Syrup
Shake well
Strain into Tumbler with shaved ice
Decorate with Fruit

Terry Sloan Cooler

1 jigger Dry Gin
⅓ jigger Crème de Cassis
1 spoon Lemon Juice
1 dash Sugar Syrup
Shake well
Strain into Tumbler
Fill with Seltzer

Vanilla Cooler

1 jigger Cognac
1 pony Crème de Vanilla
1 spoon Sugar Syrup
2 jiggers Sweet Cream
Shake well
Strain into Goblet
Grate Nutmeg over top

Cups

Champagne Cup — No. 1

(Use Large Punch Bowl)
2 jiggers Pineapple Syrup
6 sprigs Mint
1 quart Curacao
1 pint Green Chartreuse
1 quart Cognac
1 quart Tokay
3 quarts Apollinaris
6 Oranges
2 Lemons, sliced
Stir well — let ferment two hours
Strain into clean bowl and add:
½ Sliced Pineapple
½ box halved Strawberries
6 fifths Champagne
Set on ice and let stand
Stir well before using

Champagne Cup — No. 2

(Use in Pitcher)
Place in Pitcher
1½ ponies Brandy
1 pony Benedictine
1 pony Maraschino
1 bottle Soda
1 fifth Champagne
1 stick of ice
Dress with Fruit and Mint

Cider Cup

(4 People)
Use small glass jug and add:
1 pony Maraschino
1 pony Curacao
1 pony Brandy
1 quart Cider
4 lumps ice
1 split Soda Water
Stir and dress with Fruit

Claret Cup

(4 People)
Place in Pitcher
½ spoon Sugar
1½ ponies Brandy
1 pony Benedictine
1 pony Maraschino
1 glass Seltzer
Stir — add 1 stick ice
1 fifth Claret
Decorate with Fruit and Mint

Claret Cup

(20 People)
Use Large Bowl
3 fifths Claret
½ fifth Curacao
1 pint Dry Sherry
1 pint Cognac
2 jiggers Raspberry Syrup
3 Oranges, sliced
1 Lemon, sliced
6 sprigs Mint
2 fifths Seltzer
3 fifths Club Soda
Stir well — sweeten with Sugar
Strain — then ice well

Moselle Cup

Place in Pitcher
1 pint Moselle
1 pint Club Soda
1 jigger Sherry
1 pony Brandy
1 pony Anisette
3 slices Pineapple
Rind of one Lemon
Sweeten to taste
Add ice
Decorate with Fruit

Peach Cup

Use Punch Bowl
Peel two Ripe Peaches and slice
Place in bowl and add ⅕ Moselle
3 tablespoons Sugar
Stir well — let stand 30 minutes
Add ⅕ Chilled Moselle
At serving, add ⅕ Moselle Sparkling Wine and surround cup with ice

Rhine Wine Cup

Place in Pitcher
2 ponies Brandy
Cracked ice
1 pony Curacao (Orange)
1 pony Maraschino
1 quart Rhine Wine
½ pint Club Soda
Decorate with Fruit
1 piece Cucumber Peel
Several sprigs Fresh Mint
Stir well and serve

Smashes

Brandy Smash — No. 1

2 sprigs Mint
2 spoons Water
¼ spoon Sugar
   (Muddle)
Add in Fizz Glass
1 jigger Brandy
2 lumps ice
Stir and serve with spoon

Whiskey Smash

3 sprigs Mint
Fill mixing glass with ice
Add 2 more sprigs Mint
¼ spoon Sugar
½ pony Water
1 jigger Whiskey
Stir well
Strain into Fizz Glass
Dress with Fruit and Mint

Brandy Smash — No. 2

2 dashes Benedictine
2 teaspoons Powdered Sugar
1 pony Water
3 sprigs Mint
Muddle in Fizz Glass
Add one jigger Brandy
Stir and serve

Sours

Applejack Sour

Use Large Bar Glass
2 teaspoons Sugar
3 dashes Lemon Juice
1 jigger Applejack
Shake well with ice
Strain into Sour Glass
Dress with Fruit and serve

Champagne Sour

Use Large Bar Glass
1 teaspoon Powdered Sugar
3 dashes Lemon Juice
⅓ Shaved Ice
Fill with Champagne
Stir well
Dress with Fruit

Brandy Sour

Juice ½ Lemon
½ spoon Sugar
1 jigger Brandy
Shake with ice
Strain into Sour Glass
Dress with Fruits and serve

Whiskey Sour

Juice of ½ Lemon
½ spoon Sugar
½ pony Water
1 jigger Whiskey
Shake well
Strain into Sour Glass
Decorate with Fruit

Rickies

Applejack Rickey

¾ jigger Applejack
1 spoon Grenadine
1 spoon Brandy
1 spoon Lemon Juice
Stir in medium glass
Fill with Seltzer
Decorate with Fruit

Bacardi Rickey — No. 2

1 jigger Rum
1 spoon Lemon Juice
1 spoon Maraschino
Stir well in Rickey Glass
Fill with Seltzer
Decorate with Fruit

Bacardi Rickey — No. 1

¾ jigger Rum
1 jigger Benedictine
1 spoon Grenadine
1 spoon Lemon Juice
Stir well in Rickey Glass
Fill with Seltzer
Decorate with Fruit

Brandy Rickey

¾ jigger Brandy
1 spoon Maraschino
1 spoon Rum
1 spoon Lemon Juice
Stir well in Rickey Glass
Add Seltzer to fill
Decorate with Fruit

Gin Rickey

2 jiggers Dry Gin
Juice ½ Lime
1 spoon Sugar Syrup
Crush Lime in Rickey Glass
Add ice cube
Fill with Seltzer

Lime Rickey

1 jigger Dry Gin
1 spoon Grenadine
Juice ½ Lime
Stir well in Rickey Glass
Fill with Seltzer
Decorate with Fruit

Whiskey Rickey

¾ jigger Whiskey
1 spoon Maraschino
1 spoon Brandy
1 spoon Lemon Juice
Stir well in Rickey Glass
Fill with Seltzer
Decorate with Fruit

Cobblers

Brandy Cobbler

1 jigger Brandy
1 spoon Lemon Juice
1 spoon Curacao
1 spoon Sugar Syrup
Stir well
Strain into Highball Glass
Add Maraschino Cherry

Champagne Cobbler—No. 2

1 pony Brandy
1 pony Curacao
1 spoon Lemon Juice
Stir all, except Champagne
Strain into tall Highball Glass
Fill with shaved ice
Add Champagne to fill
Decorate with Fruit

Champagne Cobbler—No. 1

2 jiggers Champagne
1 spoon Sugar Syrup
Stir with ice
Strain into Highball Glass
Fill with shaved ice
Decorate with Fruit

Claret Cobbler

1 spoon Sugar Syrup
Claret to fill
Stir a little Claret with Sugar in
    Highball Glass
Fill with shaved ice
Claret to fill
Decorate with Fruit

Coffee Cobbler

1 jigger Brandy
1 pony Port
Stir well
Strain into Highball Glass
Fill with shaved ice
Twist Lemon Peel over top

Sherry Cobbler — No. 1

1½ jiggers Sherry
1 spoon Port Wine
1 spoon Curacao
Stir well in Highball Glass
Fill with shaved ice
Dash Port over top

English Cobbler

1 jigger Rum
1 spoon Lemon Juice
1 pony strong Tea
1 spoon Sugar Syrup
Stir well
Strain into Highball Glass
Fill with shaved ice
Twist Lemon Peel over top

Sherry Cobbler — No. 2

1 spoon Sugar Syrup
Sherry to fill
Stir a little Sherry with the Sugar
    in a Highball Glass
Add cracked ice to fill
Add Sherry to fill
Twist Lemon Peel over top
Decorate with Fruit

Rum Cobbler

1 jigger Jamaica Rum
1 spoon Pineapple Juice
1 spoon Bacardi Rum
Stir well
Fill with shaved ice
Twist Lemon Peel over top

Whiskey Cobbler

1 jigger Whiskey
1 spoon Sugar Syrup
Stir Whiskey with Syrup in Highball
    Glass
Add shaved ice to fill
Twist Lemon Peel over top
Decorate with Fruit

Narragansett Cobbler

Spiral peel of one Orange in Collins
    Glass
Juice of one Orange
1 jigger Whiskey
1 spoon Sugar Syrup
1 split Ginger Ale
Stir well
Decorate with Fruit

White Cobbler

1 jigger Sugar Syrup
White Wine to fill
Stir a little Wine with Syrup in
    Highball Glass
Add cracked ice to fill — White
    Wine
Decorate with Fruit

Fizzes

Alabama Fizz

Juice of ½ Lemon
½ tablespoon Powdered Sugar
1 jigger Dry Gin
Shake well
Strain into medium glass
Fill with Soda
Add 2 sprigs Mint

Apple Blow Fizz

White of one Egg
4 dashes Lemon Juice
1 teaspoon Powdered Sugar
1 jigger Calvados
Shake well
Strain into medium glass
Fill with Soda

Baltimore Fizz

½ pony Anisette
½ pony Brandy
White of one Egg
Frappe well
Fill from siphon
Serve in Fizz Glass

Bayard Beauty Fizz

1 dash Raspberry Syrup
1 dash Maraschino Liqueur
1 spoon Lemon Juice
1 jigger Old Tom Gin
Shake well
Strain into Collins Glass
Fill with Seltzer,

Chicago Fizz

Juice of ¼ Lemon
½ spoon Sugar
White of one Egg
½ jigger Jamaica Rum
½ jigger Port Wine
Shake well
Strain into Fizz Glass
Fill with Seltzer

Diamond Fizz

1½ jiggers Dry Gin
2 spoons Sugar
2 spoons Lemon Juice
Shake well
Strain into Goblet
Fill with Champagne

Dubonnet Fizz

Juice of ½ Orange
Juice of ½ Lemon
1 pony Cherry Brandy
1½ jiggers Dubonnet
Shake well
Strain into Highball Glass
Fill with Soda

France Fizz

1 jigger Cognac
1 spoon Pernod's
1 spoon Lemon Juice
1 spoon Curacao
1 spoon Grenadine
Shake well
Strain into Goblet
Fill with Seltzer

California Fizz

1 jigger Southern Comfort
¾ jigger Orange Juice
1 teaspoon Lemon Juice
1 cube of Sugar
Shake well
Strain into Fizz Glass
Fill with Soda

Gin Fizz

Juice ½ Lemon
½ spoon Sugar
1 jigger Old Tom Gin
Shake well
Strain into Goblet
Fill from siphon

Golden Fizz

Juice ½ Lemon
½ spoon Sugar
Yolk of one Egg
1 jigger Dry Gin
Shake well
Strain into Fizz Glass
Fill with Seltzer

Oral Fizz

Juice of ½ Lemon
1 spoon Sugar
1 pony Jamaica Rum
1 pony Port Wine
White of one Egg
Shake well
Strain into Fizz Glass
Fill with Seltzer

M. J. G. Fizz

Juice ½ Lemon
1 spoon Sugar
½ jigger Rye Whiskey
½ jigger Port Wine
White of one Egg
Frappé well
Strain into Fizz Glass
Fill with Seltzer
1 slice Pineapple

Ramos New Orleans Fizz

Juice ½ Lemon
½ tablespoon Powdered Sugar
White of one Egg
1 jigger Dry Gin
3 dashes Orange Flower Water
1 teaspoon Sweet Cream
Shake well
Strain into Fizz Glass
Fill with Soda

Morning Glory Fizz

Juice of ½ Lemon
½ spoon Sugar
White of one Egg
1 jigger Scotch Whisky
2 dashes Pernod's
Shake well
Strain into Fizz Glass
Fill with Seltzer

Regal Fizz

1 jigger Brandy
1 pony Benedictine
2 spoons Lemon Juice
2 spoons Sugar Syrup
Shake well
Strain into Fizz Glass
Fill with Soda

Royal Fizz

Juice ½ Lemon
½ spoon Sugar
1 jigger Old Tom Gin
1 whole Egg
Shake well
Strain into Fizz Glass
Fill with Seltzer

Fuzzy Fizz

1 jigger Crème de Menthe
1 pony Cream
Shake well
Strain into Goblet
Fill with Seltzer

180

New Orleans Fizz

Juice 1½ Lemons
White of one Egg
1 spoon Sugar
3 dashes Orange Flower Water
1 jigger Sweet Cream
1 jigger Dry Gin
Shake well
Strain into Fizz Glass

Sloe Gin Fizz

2 jiggers Sloe Gin
2 spoons Lemon Juice
1 dash Angostura
2 spoons Sugar
Shake well
Strain into Fizz Glass

Silver Fizz

Juice ½ Lemon
½ spoon Sugar
½ jigger Old Tom Gin
White of one Egg
Shake well
Strain into Fizz Glass

Texas Fizz

1½ jiggers Dry Gin
2 spoons Orange Juice
1 spoon Grenadine
1 spoon Lemon Juice
Shake well
Strain into Fizz Glass
Fill with Seltzer

Other Coles Practical, Helpful, 'How To' Books

PET CARE

Cat Care A to Z 3.95
Caring For Your Cat 2.95
Dogs — Choosing, Training
    and Care 2.50
Caring For Your Puppy 2.95
Dog Care 2.50
Dog Care A to Z 3.95
Training Your Dog 1.95
Dog Breeding For Fun and Profit 2.50
All About Aquariums 2.50
The Complete Home Aquarium .. 2.95
All About Goldfish 2.95
Tropical Fish 1.95
Canaries & Budgies 2.50

GARDENING

Indoor Gardening 3.95
Healthy House Plants 3.95
Little Plants for Small Places 2.50
Indoor Plants A to Z 3.95
Bonsai 2.95
Cacti & Succulents 2.95
Artificial Light Gardening
    Indoors 4.25
Gardening Under Glass 4.95
Hydroponics 3.95
Gardening Indoors & Outdoors 2.95
Lawn and Garden Hints 1.95
Garden Planning 2.95
Garden Secrets 4.95
Container Gardening 3.95
Rock Gardening 2.95
Growing Trees and Shrubs 4.95
Geraniums 2.50
Growing Hardy Perennials 2.95
Vegetable Gardening 2.95
Growing Food the Natural Way 2.50
Vegetables From Garden to
    Table 2.50
Garden Vegetables All Year
    'Round 3.95
How to Grow & Use Herbs 4.95

COOKERY

Quick and Easy Meals 2.50
Meals in Minutes 2.50
The 15 Minute a Day Cookbook 2.50
Handy Guide to Home Canning,
    Freezing & Preserving 3.95
Home Canning Made Easy 2.95
Home Freezing 2.50
Microwave Magic 3.95
Blender & Mixer Cooking 2.50
Apple Recipes A to Z 3.95
Guide to Cheeses of the World .. 2.95
Fondue Recipes & Cheese Dishes 2.50
Baking Bread The Easy Way 2.95

Diabetic Cookbook 4.95
Hamburgers — Plain & Fancy 2.50
Cooking With Herbs & Spices 1.95
Cooking For One 2.50
Cooking For Two 2.50
No Cooking Required 2.95
Meatless Cooking 3.95
Health Food Cooking 2.95
Chinese Cooking 2.50
French & Italian Cookery 2.50
Old Canadian Recipes 2.95
Prize Canadian Recipes 2.95
Purity Flour Canadian Cookbook 3.95

COCKTAILS, WINES, WINE AND BEER MAKING

All About Wines and Spirits 3.95
The Art of Mixing Drinks 2.50
1001 Cocktails in a Shake 2.95
Booth's Handbook of Cocktails
    & Mixed Drinks 3.95
Wines of the World 3.95
Wine & Beer Making Made Easy 2.50
Home Winemaking 2.95
Wine Recipes 2.95
Brew Your Own Beer 2.50

MEDICAL AND HEALTH

Calorie — Carbohydrate Counter 1.75
Start Counting Calories
    & Carbohydrates 3.50
Eat and Stay Slim 1.95
Diet Without Starving 1.95
Ed Allen Exercise Book 3.95
Exercises For Fitness & Health .. 3.50
Yoga 2.95
Be Healthy With Yoga 2.50
Yoga For Health & Beauty 2.95
Childbirth & Baby's First Year .. 1.95
Home Medical Guide 1.95

OCCULT

Astrology 2.95
Astrology & Palmistry 2.50
Dreams, Stars & Numerology 1.95
Meaning of Dreams 2.95

BUSINESS

Guide to Canadian Business Law 4.95
Canadian Business Law 1.95
Accounting Simplified For
    Non-Accountants 4.95
Basic Business Accounting 2.95
Dictionary of Business Terms 2.95

How To Write Better
  Business Letters 3.95
Better Letters & Reports 1.95
Business Meetings That Work 4.95
Buying or Selling Real Estate
  in Ontario 2.95

REFERENCE

4004 Names For Your Baby 2.50
Baby Names — Common
  & Uncommon 1.95
Amortized Mortgage Tables
  to 12% 2.50
Amortized Mortgage Tables
  to 25% 2.50
Teach Yourself Typing 2.95
Business Typing Simplified 2.95
Buying a House 5.95
All About Weddings & Etiquette 2.95
Guide to Marriage, Divorce &
  Family Law in Canada 4.95
Get The Job You Want 2.95
How to be a Good Secretary 4.95
Increase Your Memory 2.50
Develop Your Speed Reading
  Power 2.95
Write and Speak Clearly 1.95
Good Writing and Speaking 1.25
Dynamic Public Speaking 4.95
Self Analysis Through
  Handwriting 2.50
Hypnotism 2.95
Make The Most of Your
  Calculator 3.95
Quick and Easy Practical
  Mathematics 2.95
How to Use the Slide Rule 1.95
Understanding the Slide Rule 1.95
Instant Shorthand 2.95
Word Power Made Easy 1.95
More Word Power Made Easy 1.25
Dictionary of Synonyms
  & Antonyms 1.95
Spelling Dictionary 1.95
Correct Spelling Dictionary 2.95
Dictionary of Poetical Terms 1.25
Dictionary of Literary Terms 2.50

TECHNICAL AND
DO-IT-YOURSELF BOOKS

Car Care & Repair 6.95
First Aid For Your Car 2.95
How To Fix Almost Anything .. 4.95
Home Repairs Simplified 2.95
Fix It Yourself 3.50
First Aid For Your House 2.95
Basic Carpentry 2.95

Carpentry & Woodwork At Home 3.95
Woodworking, Painting
  & Finishing 2.50
Tools & How To Use Them 3.95
How To Use Power Tools 2.95
Home Insulation Step by Step 2.95
Plumbing Repairs Made Easy 2.95
How to Build Kitchen Cabinets .. 4.95
How to Build Wood Frame
  Houses & Summer Homes 3.95
Home Building Step by Step 4.95
Repairing & Refinishing Furniture 2.95
Repairing & Restoring Upholstery
  & Soft Furnishings 2.50
Picture Framing Made Easy 1.95
Repairing & Restoring China 1.25

CRAFTS AND HOBBIES

The Complete Guide to
  Photography 4.95
Basic Photography 2.95
Photography in a Snap 2.95
Macrame — Step By Step 2.95
Macrame & Weaving 2.50
Crochet 2.95
Knitting 2.95
Weaving 2.50
Needlecraft 1.95
Lacemaking 2.50
Tie-Dyeing, Batik & Other Crafts 1.95
Instant Sewing 2.50
Sewing Made Easy 2.95
Dressmaking 2.95
How to Draw & Paint 2.95
You Can Draw & Paint 2.50
Pottery Made Easy 2.50
Pottery Making & China
  Painting 2.50
The Art of Enamelling & Mosaics 2.50
How to Arrange Dried &
  Fresh Flowers 2.50
Wood Carving 2.50

ANTIQUES

Canadian Collector 3.95
Collecting Antique Furniture &
  Old Silver 2.50
Undiscovered Antiques 1.95
Antique Silver Hallmarks 3.95
Collector's Handbook of
  Hallmarks on Gold &
  Silver Plate 1.95

GAMES

Teach Yourself Chess 2.50
Two Weeks to Winning Chess 3.50
Chess for Beginners 2.50

How to Play Chess	2.95	How to Play Soccer	3.95
Play Winning Chess	2.50	Power Karate: Illustrated	2.95
Chess Strategy	3.50	Karate	3.95
Instant Bridge	2.50	Basic Judo	2.95
Bridge Basics	3.95	Judo	3.95
How to Play Bridge	2.50	Judo in Action	2.50
Play Winning Bridge	3.50	Complete Guide to Judo	4.95
Card Tricks Anyone Can Do	2.95	Self Defense By Judo	2.50
Magic Tricks You Can Do	3.95	How to Play Hockey	3.95
Hoyle's Card Games	3.95	Learn to Ski	3.95
Play Poker & Win	2.95	How to Ski	4.95
Las Vegas Guide to Craps,		Track & Field Know How	3.95
Blackjack & Card Games	2.50	Shape Up For Sports	3.95
Play Backgammon	2.95		
Win at Backgammon	2.50		
Play Winning Scrabble	2.95		
Scrabble Word Guide & Play	3.95		
The Complete Crossword Solver	4.95		

SPORTS

METRICS

Mini Metric Converter	1.25
Easy to Use Metric	
Conversion Tables	1.95
Handy Metric Conversion Tables	1.50
Metric Manual	1.95

How to Play Tennis	2.95
Play Tennis	3.95
Tips for Better Tennis	2.50
Winning Tennis	3.95
Teach Yourself Golf	2.50
Learn to Play Golf	3.95
Starting Squash	2.95
Play Squash	3.95
Winning Squash	2.95
Bicycling For Fitness & Fun	3.95
Bicycle Care & Repair	4.95
How to Play Snooker	3.95
Play Snooker	3.95
Fishing for Everyone	2.95
Learn to Swim	3.95
Swimming Made Easy	2.50
Horseback Riding Simplified	2.50
Riding	3.95
Horse Sense	4.95
Play The Horses & Win	2.95
Beginner's Guide to Sailing	3.50
Sailing	3.95
Sailing Skills	4.95
Knots and How to Tie Them	3.95
Teach Yourself Table Tennis	3.95
Play Table Tennis	3.95
How to Play Badminton	2.50
Teach Yourself Badminton	3.95
Winning Badminton	3.95

LANGUAGE

French for Travellers	2.50
Conversational French Made	
Easy	4.95
Sorbonne French-English/	
English-French Dictionary	2.95
French Grammar Simplified	2.95
French Verbs Simplified	2.50
How to Use French Verbs	3.95
German For Travellers	2.50
German Grammar Simplified	1.95
Italian for Travellers	2.50
Spanish for Travellers	2.50

SCIENCE

The Microscope &	
How To Use It	3.95
Exploring Outer Space	3.95

MUSIC

Teach Yourself Piano	2.95

Prices subject to change without notice.

Published by
Coles Publishing Co. Ltd.,
Toronto, Canada.